The Essential CALVIN AND HOBBES

A Calvin and Hobbes Treasury

Bill Watterson

Andrews and McMeel A Universal Press Syndicate Company Kansas City

Calvin and Hobbes is distributed internationally by Universal Press Syndicate.

 For information write Andrews and McMeel, a Universal Press Syndicate Company, 4520 Main Street, Kansas City, Missouri 64111.

ISBN: 0-8362-1809-4 (hardback)
0-8362-1805-1 (paperback)
Library of Congress Catalog Card Number: 88-71105 (hardback)
88-71106 (paperback)

98 99 00 01 BAM 20 19 18 17 16

Foreword

Bill Watterson draws wonderful bedside tables. I admire that. He also draws great water splashes and living room couches and chairs and lamps and yawns and screams, and all the things that make a comic strip fun to look at. I like the thin little arms on Calvin and his shoes that look like dinner rolls.

Drawing in a comic strip is infinitely more important than we may think, for our medium must compete with other entertainments, and if a cartoonist does nothing more than illustrate a joke, he or she is going to lose.

Calvin and Hobbes, however, contains hilarious pictures that cannot be duplicated in other mediums. In short, it is fun to look at, and that is what has made Bill's work such an admirable success.

—Charles M. Schulz

To Tom

A NAUSEOUS NOCTURNE
Another night deprived of slumber,
Hours passing without number,
My eyes trace 'round the room. I lay
Dripping sweat and now quite certain
That tonight the final curtain
Drops upon my short life's precious play.

From the darkness, by the closet
Comes a noise, much like a faucet
Makes: a madd'ning drip-drip-dripping sound.
It seems some ill-proportioned beast,
Anticipating me deceased,
Is drooling poison puddles on the ground.

A can of Mace, a forty-five,
Is all I'd need to stay alive,
But no weapon lies within my sight.

Oh my gosh! A shadow's creeping,
Ominous and black, it's seeping
Slowly 'cross a moonlit square of light!

Suddenly a floorboard creak
Announces the bloodsucking freak
Is here to steal my future years away!
A sulf'rous smell now fills the room
Heralding my imm'nent doom!
A fang gleams in the dark and murky gray!

Oh, blood-red eyes and tentacles!
Throbbing, pulsing ventricles!
Mucus-oozing pores and frightful claws!
Worse, in terms of outright scariness,
Are the suckers multifarious
That grab and force you in its mighty jaws!

This disgusting aberration
Of nature needs no motivation
To devour helpless children in their beds.
Relishing despairing moans,
It chews kids up and sucks their bones,
And dissolves inside its mouth their li'l heads!

SCARY DEATH
I know this 'cause I read it not
Two hours ago, and then I got
The heebie-jeebies and these awful shakes.
My parents swore upon their honor
That I was safe, and not a goner.
I guess tomorrow they'll see their sad mistakes.

In the morning, they'll come in
And say, "What was that awful din
We heard last night? You kept us both from sleep!"
Only then will they surmise
The gruesomeness of my demise
And see that my remains are in a heap.

Dad will look at Mom and say,
"Too bad he had to go that way."
And Mom will look at Dad, and nod assent.
Mom will add, "Still, it's fitting,
That as he was this world quitting,
He should leave another mess before he went."

They may not mind at first, I know.
They will miss me later, though,
And perhaps admit that they were wrong.
As memories of me grow dim,
They'll say, "We were too strict with him.
We should have listened to him all along."

As speedily my end approaches,
I bid a final "buenas noches"
To my best friend here in all the world.
Gently snoring, whiskers seeming
To sniff at smells (he must be dreaming),
He lies snuggled in the blankets, curled.

HEY!
HEY! WAKE UP, YOU STUPID CRETIN!
YOU GONNA SLEEP WHILE I GET EATEN?!
Suddenly the monster knows I'm not alone!
zZZ
There's an animal in bed with me!
An awful beast he did not see!
The monster never would've come if he had known!

The monster, in his consternation,
Demonstrates defenestration,
And runs and runs and runs and runs away.

Z
Rid of the pest,
I now can rest,
Thanks to my best friend, who saved the day.

The End.

SO LONG, POP! I'M OFF TO CHECK MY TIGER TRAP!
I RIGGED A TUNA FISH SANDWICH YESTERDAY, SO I'M **SURE** TO HAVE A TIGER BY NOW!
WATTERSON
THEY LIKE TUNA FISH, HUH?
TIGERS WILL DO **ANYTHING** FOR A TUNA FISH SANDWICH!
WE'RE KIND OF STUPID THAT WAY.
MUNCH MUNCH

SO DAD, WHAT DO I DO WHEN I CATCH A TIGER?
BRING IT HOME AND STUFF IT, CALVIN! CAN'T YOU SEE I'M BUSY?
SHEESH.
WATTERSON
NO, REALLY, I COULDN'T EAT ANOTHER BITE!

WHAT'S ALL THIS NOISE? YOU'RE SUPPOSED TO BE ASLEEP!
IT WAS HOBBES, DAD! HE WAS JUMPING ON THE BED! HONEST!
"HOBBES" WAS ***NOT*** JUMPING ON THE BED! NOW GO TO SLEEP!
YOU WERE **TOO** JUMPING ON THE BED!
WELL, **YOU** WERE THE ONE PLAYING THE CYMBALS!!
WATTERSON

SHOW AND TELL IS OVER, CALVIN. PLEASE PUT YOUR "TIGER" IN YOUR LOCKER.
IN MY LOCKER?! HE'LL SUFFOCATE!
WELL, AT LEAST PUT HIM UNDER YOUR CHAIR.
WHEW! THAT WAS A CLOSE ONE!
I'LL SAY!
WATTERSON
SEVEN PLUS THREE.
SEVENTY-THREE.

GOOD NIGHT, CALVIN.
'NIGHT, DAD!
HEY! AREN'T YOU GOING TO SAY GOOD NIGHT TO HOBBES?!
GOOD NIGHT, HOBBES.
THAT'S IT?! NO STORY? NO SMOOCH?!?
GO TO SLEEP, YOU SISSY.
WATTERSON

WHAT'S THIS?
TASTE IT. YOU'LL LOVE IT.
YOU KNOW YOU'LL HATE SOMETHING WHEN THEY WON'T TELL YOU WHAT IT IS.
WATTERSON

Calvin and Hobbes
by WATTERSON
OUTRAGE! WHY SHOULD I GO TO BED? I'M NOT TIRED! IT'S ONLY 7:30! THIS IS TYRANNY! I'M
ZZZZ
GOOD NIGHT, CALVIN.
WILL YOU CHECK FOR MONSTERS UNDER THE BED?
NO MONSTERS. YOU'RE SAFE.
WHAT ABOUT IN THE DRESSER?
WATTERSON
CALVIN, I'M SURE THERE ARE NO MONSTERS IN YOUR DRESSER. GO TO SLEEP.
GREAT. I'LL BET THAT'S WHERE THEY ALL ARE. THEY'LL COME OUT AND KILL US AS SOON AS WE FALL ASLEEP.
SO WHO'S GOING TO FALL ASLEEP?
WELL, WE'LL JUST HAVE TO GET THE MONSTERS FIRST. YOU IRRITATE THEM WITH THIS HORN, AND I'LL NAIL 'EM WITH MY DART GUN WHEN THEY COME OUT!
GET READY! I HEAR ONE COMING!
HONK HONK HONK HONK HONK
WHAT'S ALL THE NOISE?!
AAIEEE!! A MONSTER IN THE HALLWAY!!
DEAR, WILL YOU COME UP HERE A MINUTE?
I THINK I WOUNDED HIM. GIVE ME THE BAT AND I'LL FINISH HIM OFF!

ANY MONSTERS UNDER MY BED TONIGHT?!
NOPE!
NO!
UH-UH.
WELL, THERE'D BETTER **NOT** BE! I'D HATE TO HAVE TO **TORCH** ONE WITH MY FLAME THROWER!
YOU HAVE A FLAME THROWER??
THEY LIE. I LIE.
WATTERSON

MOM, CAN I DRIVE ON THE WAY BACK?
OF COURSE NOT, CALVIN.
CAN I JUST STEER THEN? I PROMISE I WON'T CRASH.
NO, CALVIN.
CAN I WORK THE GAS AND BRAKES WHILE **YOU** STEER?
NO, CALVIN.
WATTERSON
YOU NEVER LET ME DO ANYTHING.

HERE WE FIND A THRIVING CITY: BRAND NEW BUILDINGS, A BUSTLING ECONOMY.
A SCENIC THOROUGHFARE WINDS THROUGH THIS HAPPY MUNICIPALITY. HERE, A FARMER DRIVES HIS LIVESTOCK TO MARKET.
WATTERSON
TRAGICALLY, THIS SERENE METROPOLIS LIES DIRECTLY BENEATH THE HOOVER DAM...

THIS SMELLS LIKE BAT BARF!
THAT DOES IT, YOUNG MAN! YOU ARE EXCUSED TO YOUR ROOM!
DON'T YOU THINK THAT'S A LITTLE HARSH, DEAR? HE'LL GET HUNGRY.
CALVIN HAS GOT TO LEARN SOME MANNERS! HE WON'T STARVE TO DEATH.
...AND EXTRA PEPPERONI!

WE'LL SEE WHAT THE PRINCIPAL HAS TO SAY ABOUT YOUR ATTENTION SPAN, YOUNG MAN!
THE VALIANT SPACEMAN SPIFF HAS BEEN CAPTURED!
THE ALIENS DOUBTLESSLY WANT THE SECRET FORMULA TO THE ATOMIC NAPALM NEUTRALIZER!
MOMENTS FROM THE TORTURE CHAMBER, SPIFF SPRINGS INTO **ACTION**!
WHY IS HE EATING HIS HALL PASS?

DO YOU BELIEVE IN FATE?
YOU MEAN, THAT OUR LIVES ARE PREDESTINED?
YEAH... THAT THE THINGS WE DO ARE INEVITABLE.
WHAT A SCARY THOUGHT!

Calvin and Hobbes
by WATTERSON
NO!
NO!
NO NO NO NO NO NO
GOODNESS, WHAT WAS ALL THAT FUSS?
OH, CALVIN DIDN'T WANT TO TAKE HIS BATH. WHAT A NOISY KID!
I'M DOOMED. I CAN'T BELIEVE MY OWN PARENTS WOULD DO THIS TO ME!
AH-HA! I'VE GOT YOU NOW, KID!
AAUGH! HELP! QUICK! MOMMM!
HA HA HA! HAVE A DRINK!
HELLP! GURGLE BLUB
CALVIN! QUIET DOWN AND QUIT THAT SPLASHING! I DON'T WANT TO HAVE TO CLEAN THE WHOLE BATHROOM!
WATTERSON
HA! I PULLED THE PLUG! DOWN THE DRAIN WITH YOU! DIE, FIEND! DIE, DIE!!
AAARRRGHHH
DON'T TELL ME HE'S LETTING THE WATER OUT ALREADY!
BELIEVE IT, LADY.

BAD NEWS, DAD. YOUR POLLS ARE WAY DOWN.
MY POLLS?
YOU RATE ESPECIALLY LOW AMONG TIGERS AND SIX-YEAR-OLD WHITE MALES.
IF YOU WANT TO STAY "DAD," I'D SUGGEST YOU ADOPT SOME KEY PLANKS TO YOUR PLATFORM.
WATTERSON
SOME SPECIAL INTEREST GROUPS ARE IN FOR A SURPRISE.
OF THOSE POLLED, VIRTUALLY ALL FAVOR INCREASED ALLOWANCES AND THE COMMENCEMENT OF DRIVING LESSONS.

THERE'S A NEW GIRL IN OUR CLASS.
WELL! WHAT'S HER NAME?
WHO KNOWS?
IS SHE NICE?
WHO CARES? NOT ME!
WATTERSON
DO YOU *LIKE* HER??
NO!

HERE COMES THAT NEW GIRL.
HEY SUSIE DERKINS, IS THAT YOUR FACE, OR IS A 'POSSUM STUCK IN YOUR COLLAR?
I HOPE YOU SUFFER A DEBILITATING BRAIN ANEURYSM, YOU FREAK!
WATTERSON
SHE'S *CUTE*, ISN'T SHE??
GO AWAY.

HI, CALVIN. MIND IF I JOIN YOU FOR LUNCH?
YES.
WATTERSON
I HAVE SOUP TODAY. WHAT DO YOU HAVE?
A SQUID EYEBALL SANDWICH.
YOU DO NOT! DON'T BE DISGUSTING.
I LIKE TO SUCK OUT THE RETINAS.
MISS WORMWOOD!
CARE FOR A BITE? OR WERE YOU LEAVING?

YOU CAN'T COME UP HERE, SUSIE! NO GIRLS ALLOWED.
WHAT ON EARTH MAKES YOU THINK I'D WANT TO SIT IN A STUPID TREE IN THE FIRST PLACE?!?
WATTERSON
LEAVE IT TO A GIRL TO TAKE ALL THE FUN OUT OF SEX DISCRIMINATION.

WHEEEEEEEEE
HOUSTON, WE HAVE A NEGATIVE ON THAT ORBIT TRAJECTORY.
WATTERSON

Calvin and HOBBES by WATTERSON
OUR HERO, THE VALIANT SPACEMAN SPIFF, IS MAROONED ON A STRANGE WORLD...
I'LL SET MY MERTILIZER ON "DEEP FAT FRY."
CALVIN! YOU'RE NOT PAYING ATTENTION!
...WE JOIN SPACEMAN SPIFF ON THE DISTANT PLANET ZORG...
GRONK! ARGH!
ZOUNDS!
TRAPPED BY A HIDEOUS GRAKNIL, SPIFF DRAWS HIS TRUSTY ATOMIC NAPALM NEUTRALIZER!
CHEW ELECTRIC DEATH, SNARLING CUR!
BUT THE WEAPON IS USELESS! SPIFF IS DOOMED!!
OUR HERO MAKES A BREAK, AND DUCKS INTO A NEARBY CAVE!
WEEOOO! WHAT'S THAT AWFUL SMELL?
EEP!
TEACHERS LOUNGE
WHO WAS THAT?
BEATS ME, FRED.
SLAM!
WATTERSON

OH, MARY, YOU LOOK **RAVISHING** IN THAT SKIMPY NEGLIGEE!
KISS KISS
MMM...DARLING, DON'T YOU WISH WE WERE MARRIED?
BUT WE **ARE**! ...OR DID YOU MEAN TO EACH OTHER?
KISS KISS
I'VE GOT TO HAVE YOU! LET'S MURDER OUR SPOUSES!
MURDER?!--YOU SICK ANIMAL! I LOVE IT WHEN YOU TALK THAT WAY! COME HERE!
KISS KISS
SOMETIMES I THINK I LEARN MORE WHEN I STAY HOME FROM SCHOOL.
KISS KISS
WATTERSON

MOM, CAN I SET FIRE TO MY BED MATTRESS?
NO, CALVIN.
CAN I RIDE MY TRICYCLE ON THE ROOF?
NO, CALVIN.
THEN CAN I HAVE A COOKIE?
NO, CALVIN.
SHE'S ON TO ME.
WATTERSON

NO, MOM! DON'T PUT ME TO BED!
I INSTRUCTED HOBBES TO MESSILY DEVOUR ANYONE WHO BRINGS ME IN BEFORE 9 P.M.!
YOUR STUFFED TIGER IS IN THE WASHING MACHINE.
FINE TIME TO TAKE A **BATH**!
LISTEN, JUST BECAUSE **YOU** NEVER TAKE ONE...
PBTB!
WATTERSON

DID YOU WATCH THE MOVIE ON TV LAST NIGHT?
NOPE.
DID YOU WATCH THE GAME THEN?
NOPE.
DID YOU WATCH **ANY** TV LAST NIGHT?
NOPE.
THEN WHAT DID YOU WATCH?
WATTERSON

INSURANCE 50¢
INSURANCE ?? WHAT A DUMB IDEA!
WATTERSON
WHY WOULD ANYONE BUY INSURANCE FROM **YOU** ?!?
THWPING!
INSURANCE 50¢

BEEP BOOP
WATTERSON
HELLO, DAD! IT IS NOW THREE IN THE MORNING. DO YOU KNOW WHERE I AM?

Calvin and HOBBES
by WATTERSON
WE JOIN OUR HERO MEGAZORKS ABOVE PLANET GLOOB...
SPACEMAN SPIFF, CONQUEROR OF THE COSMOS, IS PURSUED BY THE HIDEOUS SCUM BEINGS OF PLANET Q-13!
SPIFF'S HYPER-FREEM DRIVE MALFUNCTIONS! THE ALIENS CLOSE IN!
SUDDENLY, A SEARING BOLT OF DEADLY FRAP RAY SLICES ACROSS THE BLACKNESS! OUR HERO IS UNFAZED.
ANOTHER BOLT! SPIFF IS HIT!!
PLOOIE!
SPIFF IS GOING DOWN! CAN HE MAKE IT?? IS THIS THE END?!?
AAAAAA
SPIFF'S ALIVE! HE MADE IT!!
WATTERSON
I'M ALIVE! HA HA HA! I KISS THE SWEET GROUND!
MAYBE YOU SHOULD PLAY ON THE SWINGS, CALVIN.

CALVIN, ARE YOU GOING TO TAKE THAT STUFFED TIGER TO SCHOOL AGAIN?
SURE.
DON'T THE KIDS MAKE FUN OF YOU?
TOMMY CHESNUTT DID ONCE, AND NOW NOBODY DOES.
WHY, WHAT HAPPENED TO TOMMY CHESNUTT?
HOBBES ATE HIM!
UGH! HE NEEDED A BATH, TOO...
WATTERSON

CALVIN! WHAT'S ALL THIS NOISE?! YOU'RE SUPPOSED TO BE ASLEEP!
MONSTERS UNDER THE BED, DAD! I WAS WHACKING ONE WITH MY BASEBALL BAT!
GOODNESS CALVIN, IT'S JUST YOUR STUFFED TIGER! YOU SHOULD PUT AWAY YOUR TOYS!
SORRY, OL' BUDDY. GOOD THING I MISSED OCCASIONALLY, HUH?
YEAH. LET ME SEE YOUR BAT A MINUTE.
WATTERSON

HERE COMES THE SPORTS CAR AT 200 MILES PER HOUR!
HERE COMES A CEMENT TRUCK! LOOK OUT!
AND HERE COMES AN INFLAMMABLE CHEMICAL TRUCK! OH NO!!
THIS OUGHT TO BE GOOD.
WATTERSON

DIG
DIG
PAT
PAT
CALVIN! WHAT ARE YOU DOING TO OUR YARD?!?
MAKING SPEED BUMPS.
WATTERSON

I WONDER WHERE WE GO WHEN WE DIE.
PITTSBURGH?
YOU MEAN IF WE'RE GOOD OR IF WE'RE BAD?
WATTERSON

WE'RE LOST AGAIN.
HA! WE'RE BRAVE EXPLORERS!
THE WORD "LOST" ISN'T EVEN IN OUR VOCABULARY!
HOW ABOUT THE WORD "MOMMY"?
MOMMMYYY!!
WATTERSON

Calvin and Hobbes
by WATTERSON
THERE! OUR FORTRESS IS COMPLETELY INDESTRUCTIBLE!
"SUNNY AND WARMER TODAY, HIGH IN THE UPPER THIRTIES..."
OUR SNOW FORT IS IMPENETRABLE!
AT THE SLIGHTEST PROVOCATION, WE'LL LET LOOSE A MERCILESS BARRAGE OF STINGING ICE!!
NONE DARE ATTACK US! WE RULE ALL!!
TOGETHER, A VERITABLE FIST OF DEFIANCE, WE STAND IMMUNE TO ANY ONSLAUGHT!
WE ARE INVINCIBLE!! WE...UH...UMM..
WATTERSON
PIFF!

HEY! WHERE'S THE STOCKING FOR HOBBES?
CALVIN
WATTERSON
WHERE'S SANTA GONNA STICK HOBBES' LOOT, IF HOBBES DOESN'T HAVE A STOCKING?!?
OKAY, OKAY... I'LL MAKE HOBBES A STOCKING. DON'T WORRY.
MAKE IT BIG, BUT NOT AS BIG AS MINE.
..."HOBBES' LOOT"??
DON'T LOOK AT ME! I'M DONE SHOPPING!

ARE YOU STILL AWAKE?
OF COURSE!
IT'S MIDNIGHT. LET'S GO!
AS SOON AS HE DROPS THE BAG DOWN, YOU GRAB IT, AND I'LL CLOSE THE FLUE!
CALVIN
HOBBES
WATTERSON

UH, HOBBES?... I FORGOT TO GET YOU A PRESENT. I DIDN'T EVEN MAKE YOU A CARD...
I'M SORRY, HOBBES. I DIDN'T MEAN TO FORGET.
IT'S OKAY, LITTLE BUDDY. I DIDN'T GET YOU ANYTHING EITHER.
WATTERSON
BUT HERE'S A TIGER HUG FOR BEING MY BEST FRIEND.
NOT SO HARD, YOU BIG SISSY. YOU SQUEEZE MY TEARS OUT.
MERRY CHRISTMAS.

HOW LONG DO YOU THINK IT IS TILL BEDTIME?
WATTERSON
OH, SIX OR SEVEN HOURS, I IMAGINE.
WHY DO YOU ASK?
WITH ANY LUCK, MOM WILL NOTICE WE'RE MISSING BY THEN.

WAP WAP WAP
CALVIN! WHAT ARE YOU **DOING** TO THE COFFEE TABLE?!?
IS THIS SOME SORT OF TRICK QUESTION, OR WHAT?
WATTERSON

HEY CALVIN, YOU WANT TO PLAY "HOUSE"?
I DON'T KNOW. HOW DO YOU PLAY?
OKAY... FIRST, YOU COME HOME FROM WORK. THEN I COME HOME FROM WORK.
WATTERSON
WE'LL GRIPE ABOUT OUR JOBS, AND THEN WE'LL ARGUE OVER WHOSE TURN IT IS TO MICROWAVE DINNER.

Calvin and Hobbes by WATTERSON
GAACKGURGLEPBTHFF
AGHPHHACKHACKPTUIPFTICKGPBHGR
VERY GRIM, CALVIN. YOU'RE STILL HAVING OATMEAL.
GURGLE
QUIT PLAYING WITH YOUR OATMEAL AND EAT IT, CALVIN!
GAGPTH! I'M FREE! BLAUGH BLORK!
ICK OOG
YAAH! DEATH TO OATMEAL!
KACHUNK!
AGH BLOOP ORG
YOU'LL NEVER ESCAPE, VILE GLOP! DIE! DIE!
ORK IG GOOK
CALVIN! QUIT... ..OH NO....
IT'S YOUR FAULT WE DIDN'T HAVE A SWEET LITTLE GIRL! YOUR STUPID CHROMOSOME!! NOT MINE!!
...I JUST LIVE HERE...
WATTERSON

IT SAYS HERE THAT BY THE AGE OF SIX ...
.. MOST CHILDREN HAVE SEEN A MILLION MURDERS ON TELEVISION.
I FIND THAT VERY DISTURBING!
IT MEANS I'VE BEEN WATCHING ALL THE WRONG CHANNELS.

I'M NOT EATING THIS GREEN STUFF. YECCHH!
GOOD IDEA, CALVIN. IT'S A PLATE OF TOXIC WASTE THAT WILL TURN YOU INTO A MUTANT IF YOU EAT IT.
!
RRGHHMPHFFG
MMMM
SCRAPE URF
GLUNK SMACK
URF YUM
THERE HAS GOT TO BE A BETTER WAY TO MAKE HIM EAT!
AHHHH.. I CAN FEEL IT WORKING..

DAD, HOW COME YOU LIVE IN THIS HOUSE WITH MOM...
.. INSTEAD OF IN AN APARTMENT WITH SEVERAL SCANTILY CLAD FEMALE ROOMMATES?
BOY! ASK A SIMPLE QUESTION, AND GET ALL YOUR TELEVISION PRIVILEGES REVOKED.

HOBBES, HAVE YOU EVER KISSED A GIRL?
A FEW, I GUESS.
REALLY? WHAT WAS IT LIKE?
MMMMMMMMM POP!
MFGHR!
...ONLY A LOT MORE SO!
GAACK! I WAS HOPING IT WOULDN'T BE SO FUZZY...
WATTERSON

WHAT DO YOU FIND ATTRACTIVE IN WOMEN, HOBBES?
WELL, I'VE ALWAYS BEEN PARTIAL TO REDHEADS.
...WITH GREEN EYES. I LIKE GREEN EYES.
...AND WHISKERS! LONG WHISKERS!
LET'S CHANGE THE SUBJECT.
WATTERSON

HAVING TRANSFORMED MYSELF INTO A WEREWOLF, I SEARCH FOR HUMAN SACRIFICE!
HI, DAD!
MM...HELLO.
CALVIN, STOP THAT DISGUSTING DROOLING!
WATTERSON

Calvin and HobbES
by WATTERSON
I LOVE WINTER DAYS. THEY'RE SO PEACEFUL.
HA HA! GOTCHA, SUSIE!
WAP!
HEY, YOU DUMMY! YOU'LL NEVER BE ABLE TO THROW A SNOW BALL THAT BIG! HA! STUPID GIRL!
HEY, WHAT ARE YOU DOING? GET AWAY.
HEY! PUT ME DOWN! WHERE ARE YOU TAKING ME?! HEY! HEY!
CHUNK
WATTERSON

ALL RIGHT, CLASS, WHO WOULD LIKE TO GIVE HIS BOOK REPORT FIRST?
CALVIN, HOW ABOUT YOU?
CALVIN?
CALVIN?
SPACEMAN SPIFF COOLY DRAWS HIS DEATH RAY BLASTER...
WATTERSON

2+7= ___
I cannot answer this qwestion, as it is against my religious principles.
IT'S WORTH A SHOT.
WATTERSON

HOBBES, WHAT DO YOU THINK HAPPENS TO US WHEN WE DIE?
I THINK WE PLAY SAXOPHONE FOR AN ALL-GIRL CABARET IN NEW ORLEANS.
SO YOU BELIEVE IN HEAVEN?
CALL IT WHAT YOU LIKE.
WATTERSON

WE ARE A FIERCE AND DIRTY BAND OF CUTTHROAT PIRATES!
KEEP A SHARP LOOKOUT, MATEY. WE WANT NO SISSY GIRLS ON OUR SHIP!
WE DON'T *LIKE* GIRLS?
OF COURSE NOT, DUMMY! WE'RE A MURDEROUS BUNCH OF *PIRATES*, REMEMBER?!
WHO DO WE SMOOCH THEN?
WATTERSON

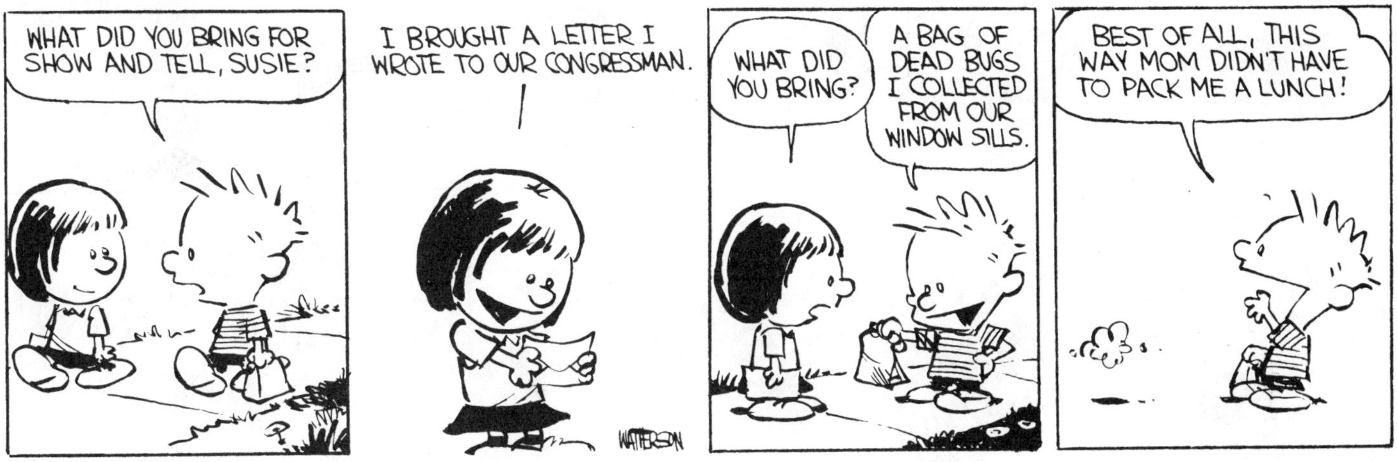
WHAT DID YOU BRING FOR SHOW AND TELL, SUSIE?
I BROUGHT A LETTER I WROTE TO OUR CONGRESSMAN.
WHAT DID YOU BRING?
A BAG OF DEAD BUGS I COLLECTED FROM OUR WINDOW SILLS.
BEST OF ALL, THIS WAY MOM DIDN'T HAVE TO PACK ME A LUNCH!
WATTERSON

WELL, HOBBES, WE DID IT AGAIN. WE'RE SEPARATED FROM THE TROOP AND HOPELESSLY LOST.
FORTUNATELY, OUR MOTTO IS "BE PREPARED."
WITH THIS FULL BACKPACK, WE CAN STAY OUT HERE FOR WEEKS!
JUST SO LONG AS WE DON'T GET HUNGRY.
COMIX
WATTERSON

Calvin and Hobbes
by WATTERSON
I'M HOME FROM SCHOOL!
SO I GATHERED.
HOBBES?
YAAAAAH!
AAAAUGH! TIGER ATTACK!
GRRRR
RRRRRRRRR
RRRRR
RRRRRR
RRR
BINK BONK BANG BOING
CALVIN! QUIT CRASHING AROUND!
HOBBES JUMPED ME, MOM! I WAS FIGHTING FOR MY VERY SURVIVAL!!
SURE, CALVIN. LOOK, I DON'T WANT TO SEW HOBBES UP AGAIN, SO WHY DON'T YOU TWO GO DO SOMETHING QUIET?
OKAY, OKAY...
YOU SISSY. MOM ALWAYS TAKES YOUR SIDE!
THAT'S BECAUSE SHE WANTED ANOTHER TIGER, NOT YOU!
WATTERSON

CALVIN, PASS THIS NOTE TO JESSICA.
IT'S A **SECRET** NOTE, SO DON'T READ IT.
WATTERSON
Calvin you stinkhead: I told you not to read this. Susie

THAT DIRTY SUSIE DERKINS. SHE'LL BE SORRY IF SHE TRIES TO PASS ANOTHER NOTE.
PSST...CALVIN! PASS THIS SECRET NOTE TO JESSICA, OKAY?
TEACHER! SUSIE'S PASSING NOTES! TAKE THIS AWAY AND READ IT IN FRONT OF THE CLASS!
"DEAR JESSICA, YOU KNOW WHAT I HATE ABOUT CALVIN? HE'S A SQUEALER! SIGNED, SUSIE."
I HOPE YOU KNOW A GOOD DENTIST, SUSIE...
WATTERSON

NOW LOOK! YOU GOT US SENT TO THE PRINCIPAL'S OFFICE!
GOSH! DO YOU THINK WE'LL GET PADDLED?!?
THEY CAN'T PADDLE ME! I'M A GIRL!!
WHAT'S **THAT** GOT TO DO WITH IT?
GIRLS HAVE MORE DELICATE HEINIES.
WATTERSON

CALVIN, I DON'T WANT TO BE SPANKED!
WHAT IF IT GOES ON OUR ACADEMIC TRANSCRIPTS? WE'LL BE RUINED!
* SNIFF *
DARN YOU, CALVIN!! YOU'RE GONNA ANSWER TO MY PARENTS IF I CAN'T GET MY MASTER'S DEGREE!
WATTERSON

CALVIN AND SUSIE, WOULD YOU COME IN MY OFFICE, PLEASE?
PRINCI
IT WAS ALL HIS FAULT, MR. SPITTLE!
THAT'S A LIE! SHE STARTED IT!
ARE YOU GOING TO SPANK US?!?
I'LL NEVER PASS NOTES AGAIN! DON'T SPANK US!!
WAAAHHHH!! I WISH WE WERE DEAD!!
I HATE THIS JOB.
WATTERSON

NOW I WANT YOU BOTH TO PAY BETTER ATTENTION IN CLASS, UNDERSTOOD?
YES SIR.
OKAY, YOU MAY RETURN TO YOUR ROOM NOW.
THANK YOU, MR. SPITTLE.
CALVIN? YOU MAY RETURN TO YOUR ROOM.
CALVIN?
THE ZORG DRAWS NEARER. SPIFF SETS HIS BLASTER ON "MEDIUM WELL"...
WATTERSON

Calvin and HOBBES
by WATTERSON
IT SAYS HERE THAT "RELIGION IS THE OPIATE OF THE MASSES." ...WHAT DO YOU SUPPOSE THAT MEANS?
..IT MEANS KARL MARX HADN'T SEEN ANYTHING YET..
WHAT ARE YOU WATCHING?
GARBAGE. THIS SHOW WOULD INSULT A 6-YEAR-OLD! AND I SHOULD KNOW.
SO WHY WATCH IT?
ALL THE OTHER SHOWS ARE EVEN WORSE!
WHY WATCH TV AT ALL THEN?
THERE'S NOTHING TO DO.
NOTHING TO DO?! YOU COULD READ A BOOK! OR WRITE A LETTER! OR TAKE A WALK!
WHEN YOU'RE OLD, YOU'LL WISH YOU HAD MORE THAN MEMORIES OF THIS TRIPE TO LOOK BACK ON.
UNDOUBTEDLY.
WATTERSON

..AND WITH THAT REPORT, WE...
CLICK
BEEEOOooooop
CLICK
RATS.
WATTERSON

MOM, CAN I TAKE UP THE FLOORBOARDS IN MY ROOM AND MAKE A SECRET PASSAGEWAY?
WATTERSON
OF COURSE NOT, CALVIN. DON'T BE RIDICULOUS.
WHY CAN'T I?
BECAUSE YOU'D COME RIGHT THROUGH THE KITCHEN CEILING. I SAID DON'T DO IT.
OKAY, OKAY...
HOW QUIETLY DO YOU THINK WE CAN NAIL THESE BACK IN?

WHAT'S THIS DISGUSTING SLIMY BLOB?
TRY IT. YOU'LL LOVE IT.
OH YEAH? WELL WHAT IF I DON'T LOVE IT?!?
THEN IT WILL BUILD CHARACTER.
WATTERSON.
THAT'S MY DAD. ALWAYS LOOKING OUT FOR ME.

CALVIN! YOU'RE GOING TO BE LATE FOR SCHOOL! GET UP!
CALVIN, IT'S ALMOST 7:30! ARE YOU UP??
I'M COMING.
SEE? I **TOLD** YOU IT WOULDN'T WORK!
OF COURSE NOT, DUMMY! YOU DIDN'T PUT ON ANY PANTS!
WATTERSON

DO YOU KNOW WHERE BABIES COME FROM?
NOPE.
WELL, I WONDER HOW ONE FINDS OUT!
...HERE, LET ME SEE THE BACK OF YOUR SHIRT.
YOU CAME FROM TAIWAN.
WATTERSON

HEY, MOM, WHEN'S LUNCH?
LATER, CALVIN. I'M BUSY.
BUT I'M HUNGRY NOW! I WANNA EAT!
A MAP TO THE REFRIGERATOR. HILARIOUS.
WATTERSON

Calvin and Hobbes
by WATTERSON
"McZARGALD'S ... NEXT EXIT... 50 MEGAZORKS.."
"..OVER 75 MILLION EARTHLINGBURGERS SERVED..."
SPACEMAN SPIFF IS GOING DOWN!!!
WE JOIN OUR HERO AS HE STRUGGLES TO LAND HIS DAMAGED SPACECRAFT!
THE ALTITUDE FLAPS REFUSE TO RESPOND, BUT FEARLESS SPIFF IS UNFAZED!
SPIFF CAREENS THROUGH THE ALIEN CANYON! IS THIS THE END ??
NO! MOMENTS BEFORE IMPACT, SPIFF EJECTS!
WATTERSON
NOW ARE YOU THROUGH CHARGING AROUND THE HOUSE, OR ARE YOU GOING TO FALL DOWN THE STAIRS AGAIN?
OUR HERO REGAINS CONSCIOUSNESS AT THE FEET OF A SARCASTIC ALIEN...

HI, DAD. IT'S ME, CALVIN!
HOW'S WORK GOING? ...UH HUH... PRETTY DAY OUT, ISN'T IT? ... YEP.....
ARE YOU BRINGING ME HOME ANY PRESENTS TONIGHT? ... NO? WELL, JUST THOUGHT I'D ASK...
LISTEN, I SUPPOSE YOU'RE WONDERING WHY I CALLED...

DAD, YOUR POLLS TOOK A BIG DIVE THIS WEEK.
YOUR "OVERALL DAD PERFORMANCE" RATING WAS ESPECIALLY LOW.
SEE? RIGHT ABOUT YESTERDAY YOUR POPULARITY WENT DOWN THE TUBES.
CALVIN, YOU DIDN'T GET DESSERT YESTERDAY BECAUSE YOU FLOODED THE HOUSE!!
I'D SUGGEST A NEW LINE OF WORK, "DAD"!...

THE GIANT SLIMY OCTOPUS OOZES ACROSS THE BEACH.
HIS HIDEOUS PRESENCE TERRORIZES THE SLEEPY WATERFRONT COMMUNITY.
WITH A SUCKER-COVERED TENTACLE, HE GRABS AN UNSUSPECTING TOURIST.
A MUFFLED SCREAM LINGERS IN THE SALTY AIR!
DID YOU WANT SOMETHING, CALVIN?
ACK
ICK
IG

UH-OH, HERE COMES MOE, THE CLASS BULLY!
Okay twinky, let's have that ball.
SURE, MOE. ALL YOURS
NEVER ARGUE WITH A SIX-YEAR-OLD WHO SHAVES.
WATTERSON

Hey! You took my favorite swing!
THAT'S TRUE, MOE. HOW ABOUT THAT?
..uh..
HIS TRAIN OF THOUGHT IS STILL BOARDING AT THE STATION.
WATTERSON

MOE, I WAS WONDERING SOMETHING.
ARE YOUR MALADJUSTED ANTISOCIAL TENDENCIES THE PRODUCT OF YOUR BERSERK PITUITARY GLAND?
WATTERSON
what?
ISN'T HE GREAT, FOLKS? LET'S GIVE HIM A BIG HAND!

Calvin and Hobbes
by WATTERSON
WHAT SHOULD WE HAVE DAD READ US TONIGHT?
..SO IN THE NEXT PANEL, SUPERTOAD GOES "PLOOIE," AND...
" 'MY, WHAT BIG TEETH YOU HAVE!' SAID LITTLE RED RIDING HOOD. 'THE BETTER TO EAT YOU WITH!' SAID THE WOLF..."
TIGER.
"...SAID THE TIGER, AND HE POUNCED ON LITTLE RED RIDING HOOD."
"JUST THEN A HUNTER CAME BY, AND WHEN HE SAW THE WOLF..."
TIGER.
"..WHEN HE SAW THE TIGER, HE PICKED UP HIS GUN AND..."
..AND?
"...AND IT WAS TOO LATE. THE TIGER ATE THEM BOTH AND HE LIVED HAPPILY EVER AFTER. THE END."
GOOD STORY, DAD! THANKS!
SNIFF I ALWAYS CRY AT HAPPY ENDINGS.
WATTERSON

"A BUSHEL IS A UNIT OF WEIGHT EQUAL TO FOUR PECKS."
WHAT'S A PECK?
A QUICK SMOOCH.
YOU KNOW, I DON'T UNDERSTAND MATH AT ALL.

MOM, CAN I HAVE SOME MONEY SO HOBBES AND I CAN GO TO A MOVIE?
WHAT MOVIE?
"THE CUISINART MURDERER OF CENTRAL HIGH."
I REALLY THINK THERE ARE MORE CONSTRUCTIVE WAYS YOU COULD SPEND YOUR AFTERNOON, CALVIN.
WHAT DID SHE SAY?
OH, SHE WENT OFF ON ONE OF HER IRRELEVANT TANGENTS AGAIN.

DO YOU BELIEVE OUR DESTINIES ARE CONTROLLED BY THE STARS?
NO, I THINK WE CAN DO WHATEVER WE WANT WITH OUR LIVES.
NOT TO HEAR MOM AND DAD TELL IT.

READY?
NO.
HURRY UP!
OKAY, I'M READY!

I HAVE A QUESTION.
DO YOU BELIEVE IN LIFE AFTER DEATH?
YOU KNOW, REINCARNATION?
YOU JUST STEER, OKAY?

MEEK AND MILD-MANNERED CALVIN DUCKS INTO A NEARBY CLOSET AND TRANSFORMS HIMSELF INTO...
CAPTAIN NAPALM
PROTECTOR OF THE AMERICAN WAY!
ENDOWED WITH SUPERHUMAN POWERS, HE QUICKLY...
MOMMMMMMM!

Calvin and HOBBES
by WATTERSON
MAN THE HARPOONS! THAR SHE BLOWS!!
CAN HOBBES TAKE A BATH TOO?
NO, HOBBES DOESN'T NEED ONE. HOLD STILL.
BY GOLLY, WHAT IF I DROWN BECAUSE NOBODY WAS HERE TO RESCUE ME?!?
HOBBES! C'MERE!
MOM CAN'T KNOW YOU'RE IN HERE, OKAY?
I'LL DISGUISE MYSELF WITH BUBBLES.
HMM.. YOU NEED A HAT. HANG ON, AND I'LL GET ONE OF DAD'S.
I LIKE HIS GRAY ONE BEST.
WATTERSON
MAYBE YOU SHOULD WEAR A TIE, TOO. I'LL BE RIGHT BACK.
BETTER HURRY! I THINK I HEAR YOUR MOM COMING!
DEAR! WHY ARE YOU TAKING A BATH?!? ... AND WEARING YOUR BEST HAT!!

WAKE UP, CALVIN. IT'S TIME FOR SCHOOL.
I'M NOT GOING TO SCHOOL ANYMORE.
YOU HAVE TO. IT'S THE LAW.
WHAT ABOUT HOBBES? WHY DOESN'T **HE** HAVE TO GO TO SCHOOL?
HE'S A TIGER. GET UP.
WHAT'S BEING A TIGER GOT TO DO WITH IT?
TIGERS WRECK THE GRADE CURVE.

DO YOU THINK IT'S BETTER TO LIVE IN STUPEFYING SECURITY...
...OR TO TAKE RISKS AND LIVE LIFE ON THE EDGE?
I THINK IT'S BETTER TO ACCEPT DANGER AND LIVE TO THE FULLEST!
I TAKE IT BY YOUR SILENCE THAT YOU AGREE...

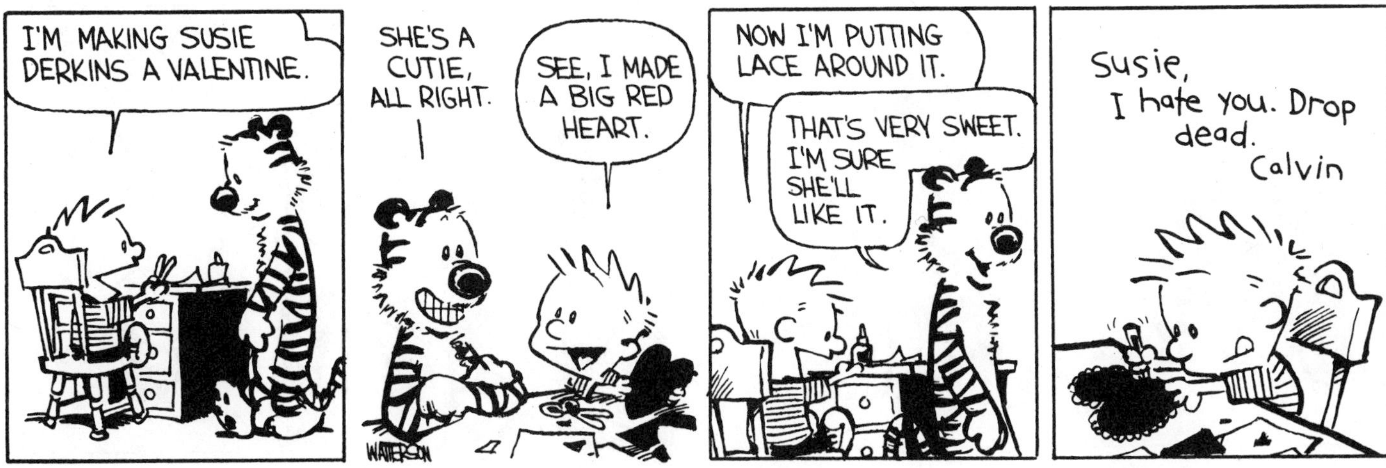
I'M MAKING SUSIE DERKINS A VALENTINE.
SHE'S A CUTIE, ALL RIGHT.
SEE, I MADE A BIG RED HEART.
NOW I'M PUTTING LACE AROUND IT.
THAT'S VERY SWEET. I'M SURE SHE'LL LIKE IT.
Susie, I hate you. Drop dead. Calvin

I'D LIKE TO GET A VALENTINE BOUQUET FOR A GIRL I KNOW.
WHAT A SWEET LITTLE BOY YOU ARE! COME SEE WHAT WE HAVE.
IS THIS ALL?
DID YOU HAVE SOMETHING SPECIAL IN MIND?
SORT OF. DO YOU HAVE A DUMPSTER OUT BACK I COULD ROOT THROUGH?
WATTERSON

CALVIN, YOU BALONEY BRAIN!
!
YOU SENT ME A HATE-MAIL VALENTINE AND A CRUMMY BUNCH OF DEAD FLOWERS!
SO HERE'S A VALENTINE FOR YOU, YOU INSENSITIVE CLOD!!
POW
A VALENTINE AND FLOWERS! HE LIKES ME!
SHE NOTICED! SHE LIKES ME!
WATTERSON

WATTERSON

Calvin and Hobbes
by WATTERSON
HEY, CALVIN! ARE WE NEAR A SLAUGHTERHOUSE, OR DID YOU FORGET YOUR DEODORANT?!
DROP DEAD, SUSIE! YOU'RE SO UGLY, I HEAR YOUR MOM PUTS A BAG OVER YOUR HEAD BEFORE SHE KISSES YOU GOODNIGHT!!
IT'S SHAMELESS THE WAY WE FLIRT.
WHAT'S IT LIKE TO FALL IN LOVE?
WELL... SAY THE OBJECT OF YOUR AFFECTION WALKS BY...
YEAH?
FIRST, YOUR HEART FALLS INTO YOUR STOMACH AND SPLASHES YOUR INNARDS.
ALL THE MOISTURE MAKES YOU SWEAT PROFUSELY.
THIS CONDENSATION SHORTS THE CIRCUITS TO YOUR BRAIN, AND YOU GET ALL WOOZY.
WHEN YOUR BRAIN BURNS OUT ALTOGETHER, YOUR MOUTH DISENGAGES AND YOU BABBLE LIKE A CRETIN UNTIL SHE LEAVES.
THAT'S LOVE?!?
WATTERSON
MEDICALLY SPEAKING.
HECK, THAT HAPPENED TO ME ONCE, BUT I FIGURED IT WAS COOTIES!!

Hey, Calvin, it's gonna cost you 50 cents to be my friend today.
AND WHAT IF I DON'T WANT TO BE YOUR FRIEND TODAY?
Then the janitor scrapes you off the wall with a spatula.
HECK, WHAT'S A LITTLE EXTORTION AMONG FRIENDS?
WATTERSON

I GOT THE NEW ALBUM BY SCRAMBLED DEBUTANTE.
ALL THEIR SONGS GLORIFY DEPRAVED VIOLENCE, MINDLESS SEX, AND THE DELIBERATE ABUSE OF DANGEROUS DRUGS.
YOUR MOM'S GOING TO GO INTO CONNIPTIONS WHEN SHE SEES THIS LYING AROUND.
WELL I SURE DIDN'T BUY IT FOR THE MUSIC..
WATTERSON

MOM, WILL YOU DRIVE ME INTO TOWN?
WHY SHOULD I DRIVE YOU, CALVIN? IT'S A PERFECT DAY OUTSIDE!
WHAT DO YOU THINK PEOPLE HAVE FEET FOR?
TO WORK THE GAS PEDAL.
WATTERSON

CALVIN, YOU'RE NOT PAYING ATTENTION AGAIN!
7 +2
SPACEMAN SPIFF, CONQUEROR OF THE COSMOS, IS TRAPPED BY A HIDEOUS ZONDARG!
WITH LIGHTNING SPEED, SPIFF BOLTS FOR THE AIR LOCK, MAKING A DARING ESCAPE!
NICE TRY, CALVIN.

I'M HOME!
DID YOU FEED HOBBES TODAY, MOM?
NO, DEAR, IT MUST HAVE SLIPPED MY MIND.
THANKS, MOM. YOU WANNA JUST DOUSE ME IN STEAK SAUCE BEFORE I GO TO MY ROOM?

MOMMMM!
I'M THIRSTY!
WHAT'S THIS? JUST WATER?

Calvin and Hobbes
by WATTERSON
HEY MOM, CAN I DRIVE NOW?
NO.
HOW ABOUT NOW?
KLUNK
OH NO!
OH YOU STUPID CAR! WHAT'S WRONG WITH YOU NOW?!?
THAT'S IT, MOM! GO AHEAD AND SWEAR! WE DON'T MIND!
CALVIN, BE QUIET!
WANT HOBBES AND ME TO GO GET HELP?
YOU STAY WHERE YOU ARE. I'LL LOOK UNDER THE HOOD.
KICK THE CAR, MOM! IT WORKS ON THE TV!
LOOK AT ALL THESE CARS GOING BY. NOBODY'S STOPPING TO HELP.
LET'S BLOW THE HORN! MAYBE SOMEONE WILL COME.
WATTERSON
BEEEEP!
AAUGH!
BEEP! BEEP!
HOORAYY!! SOMEONE STOPPED! WE'RE HEROES!!
WANT ME TO CALL A TOW TRUCK, LADY?
FIRST CALL THE POLICE AND REPORT AN INFANTICIDE.

I NEED HELP ON MY HOMEWORK. WHAT'S A PRONOUN?
A NOUN THAT LOST ITS AMATEUR STATUS.
MAYBE I CAN GET A POINT FOR ORIGINALITY.
WATTERSON

LEAVE YOUR TIGER IN THE CAR, CALVIN.
CAN'T HOBBES COME ALONG, DAD? HE WON'T EAT ANYBODY!
NO, CALVIN. LET'S GO.
WELL, AT LEAST LET ME OPEN THE WINDOW AND GIVE HIM SOME AIR.
SEE IF HE'LL LEAVE THE KEYS, TOO, SO I CAN LISTEN TO THE RADIO.
WATTERSON

CALVIN, YOUR MOTHER AND I HAVE DECIDED TO GIVE YOU AN ALLOWANCE.
IT'S IMPORTANT THAT ONE LEARNS THE VALUE OF MONEY.
MONEY! HA HA HA! I'M RICH! I'M RICH! I CAN BUY OFF ANYONE! THE WORLD IS MINE!
WATTERSON
POWER! FRIEND
PRESTIGE!
I BLEW IT AGAIN, DEAR!
I CAN BUY IT ALL! I'M FREE! HA HA HA HA!

WHEN I GROW UP, I WANT TO BE A RADICAL TERRORIST.
MM HMM..
I'M GOING TO INHALE THIS CAN OF PESTICIDE.
MM HMM..
I'M GOING TO WATCH TV ALL NIGHT.
THAT'S WHAT *YOU* THINK, BUSTER!
YOU CAN NEVER TELL IF THEY'RE LISTENING OR NOT.
WATTERSON

HERE'S A GOOD MOVIE! "VAMPIRE SORORITY BABES"!
IT SAYS YOU HAVE TO BE EIGHTEEN TO GET IN.
HECK, THAT'S NO PROBLEM! LET'S GO!
WATTERSON
THIS IS A NEW ONE.
TWO PLEASE. ...I MEAN, ONE.

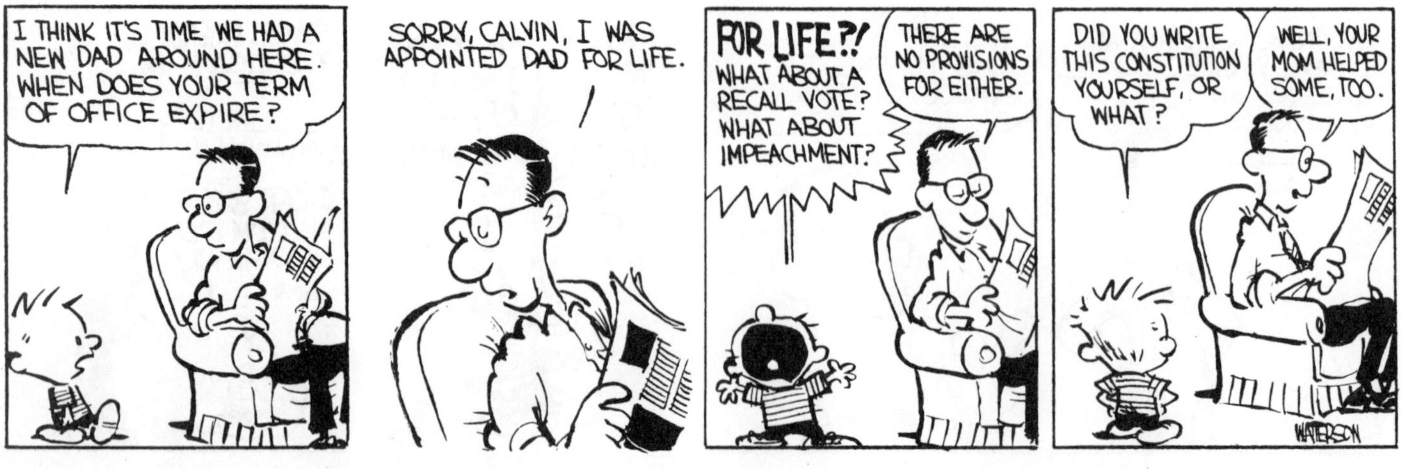
I THINK IT'S TIME WE HAD A NEW DAD AROUND HERE. WHEN DOES YOUR TERM OF OFFICE EXPIRE?
SORRY, CALVIN, I WAS APPOINTED DAD FOR LIFE.
FOR LIFE?! WHAT ABOUT A RECALL VOTE? WHAT ABOUT IMPEACHMENT?
THERE ARE NO PROVISIONS FOR EITHER.
DID YOU WRITE THIS CONSTITUTION YOURSELF, OR WHAT?
WELL, YOUR MOM HELPED SOME, TOO.
WATTERSON

Calvin and Hobbes
by WATTERSON
AACHOO!
GESUNDHEIT!
OKAY! HOW MANY MONSTERS ARE UNDER MY BED TONIGHT?
JUST ONE.
WATTERSON
THAT'S GOOD, HOBBES! WE OUTNUMBER HIM!
HEE HEE! WANNA GET HIM?
YEAH! SEE IF YOU CAN REACH THE BASEBALL BAT! HEH HEH!
QUIT SHOVING, YOU HOGS!
MOMMMMM!
NICE GOING, MAURICE.

You're gonna taste asphalt fifth period, Twinky. Just so you know.
GREAT. I'M DEAD.
FIFTH PERIOD - "STUDIES IN CONTEMPORARY STATE-SPONSORED TERRORISM."
... ALSO KNOWN AS GYM CLASS.
WATTERSON

I CAN'T GET A BABY SITTER ANYWHERE! WHAT SHOULD WE DO?
WE WON'T BE GONE LONG. COULDN'T CALVIN BE LEFT FOR A COUPLE HOURS UNSUPERVISED?
WATTERSON
HA HA HA HA HA
HO HO HO HO HEE HEE
HA
HOO HO
HO H
HAR
HA
...SERIOUSLY... WHAT SHOULD WE DO?
HEE HEE

OKAY, CALVIN, WE'LL BE BACK IN A COUPLE OF HOURS.
YOU AND HOBBES JUST WATCH TV AND BE GOOD, OKAY?
WATTERSON
DID YOU HEAR THAT? WE GET TO WATCH TV!!
HOORAY!
VIDEORAMA? I'D LIKE TO RENT A VCR AND SOME MOVIES!
ASK IF THEY HAVE "ATTACK OF THE COED CANNIBALS."

WELL, THE HOUSE IS STILL STANDING. CALVIN MUST HAVE GONE TO BED.
HIS LIGHT IS STILL ON. ... CALVIN? ARE YOU AWAKE?
EEP!
WATTERSON
DID YOU WATCH A SCARY MOVIE ?!?
NO. DON'T COME IN. THE RUG IS RIGGED TOO.

WHAP!
SMASH
TINKLE
DING
SHATTER
CLINK
WOW. FIRST TRY!
WATTERSON

WATTERSON
DOWNTOWN TOKYO!
AARRGHHGH!
GODZILLA.

Calvin and Hobbes
by WATTERSON
HOW CAN I GET SOME MONEY?
...SHORT OF EARNING IT, I MEAN...
I WANT A GRENADE LAUNCHER, MOM. WHEN'S CHRISTMAS?
NOT FOR A LONG TIME.
WHEN'S MY BIRTHDAY?
NOT FOR A LONG TIME.
WHEN'S MY ALLOWANCE?
YOU SPENT IT ALREADY.
DO I HAVE ANY STOCKS I CAN CASH? WAR BONDS??
CALVIN, I'M TRYING TO WORK!
CAN I BORROW SOME SOAP?
YES, YOU CAN BORROW SOME SOAP. HAVE ALL THE SOAP YOU WANT.
4 SaLE CHEEP!
WATTERSON

BOY, IS IT COLD!
YOU SHOULD GET A GOOD FUR COAT LIKE MINE.
WOOF! WHAT DID YOU EAT FOR BREAKFAST? CEMENT?
LOOK, WAS THIS *MY* IDEA?

OH NO, I LOST MY QUARTER!
WHERE DID YOU LOSE IT?
IT'S SOMEWHERE IN THIS FIELD.
WE'LL NEVER FIND IT. YOU'LL HAVE TO WAIT TILL THE SNOW MELTS.
TILL THE SNOW MELTS?! IT'S 25 CENTS!!
ZZZZZZZ

WANNA SEE SOMETHING WEIRD?
WATCH. YOU PUT BREAD IN THIS SLOT AND PUSH DOWN THIS LEVER...
THEN IN A FEW MINUTES, TOAST POPS UP!
DING!
WOW. WHERE DOES THE BREAD GO?
BEATS ME. ISN'T THAT WEIRD?

HOW ARE YOU TODAY?
FINE.
I WANT THE TOP OF MY HEAD SHAVED, AND THE SIDES DYED PINK AND CUT IN HORIZONTAL STRIPES, OK?
MA'AM?
GIVE HIM THE USUAL, PETE.
WELL I GUESS THIS GUY KNOWS WHICH SIDE **HIS** BREAD IS BUTTERED ON!
WATTERSON

THERE, HOW'S THAT LOOK?
THAT'S GREAT. PERFECT.
WITHOUT QUESTION, THIS IS THE FINEST HAIRCUT I HAVE EVER RECEIVED.
NEVER CRITICIZE A GUY WITH A RAZOR...
WATTERSON

TOO BAD THE WORLD WILL BE ENDING SOON.
BEG YOUR PARDON?
HALLEY'S COMET. COMETS ARE HARBINGERS OF DOOM.
WATTERSON
NO, THEY AREN'T. THAT'S JUST SUPERSTITION.
REALLY ??
GUESS I'D BETTER WRITE THAT BOOK REPORT.

Calvin and Hobbes
by WATTERSON
READY?
LET ME CHECK WHAT THE DEDUCTIBLE IS ON MY INSURANCE POLICY...
MUNCH MUNCH
WOULD YOU CARE FOR A SOFT DRINK?
OK.
H-H-HERE Y-YOU A-A-ARE!
BONK!
BONK!
BONK!
ANY DESSERT?
NO, THANKS.
WE'LL BE LANDING SHORTLY.
THE CAPTAIN HAS TURNED OFF THE SEAT BELT SIGN. THANK YOU FOR CHOOSING CALVIN'S FLIGHT 240 NON-STOP TO STONEY GULCH.
NEXT TIME I WON'T TAKE THE DINNER FLIGHT.
WATTERSON

DO YOU LOVE ME, DAD?
OF COURSE I DO, CALVIN.
WOULD YOU STILL LOVE ME IF I DID SOMETHING BAD?
WELL OF COURSE ... I ... WOULD...
I MEAN SOMETHING REALLY *REALLY*..
CALVIN, WHAT DID YOU DO?!
WATTERSON

WELL, DAD, YOUR POLLS ARE REAL HIGH THIS WEEK.
I'M GLAD TO HEAR THAT.
YEP, THOSE POLLED THINK YOU'RE DOING A FINE JOB AS DAD.
IN FACT, WITH A LITTLE PUSH TODAY, YOUR POLITICAL STOCK COULD REACH A RECORD HIGH.
WATTERSON
NICE TRY. GO HELP YOUR MOM WITH THE DISHES.
OOH DAD! SUICIDE! OOH! OOH!

HERE COMES MOE, THE CLASS BULLY.
HE'S NOT SMART, BUT HE'S STREETWISE.
THAT MEANS HE KNOWS WHAT STREET HE LIVES ON.
WATTERSON

TOLL BOOTH, DAD! YOU CAN'T PUT THE CAR IN UNTIL YOU PAY ME A QUARTER!
WHY SHOULD I PAY YOU TO PUT *MY* CAR IN *MY* GARAGE?
BECAUSE IF YOU DON'T, I'LL PULL THE DOOR DOWN ON THE HOOD AS YOU DRIVE IN!
WATTERSON
WHAT A CHEAPSKATE.

A LITTLE LOWER...OK, FINE!
THANKS FOR HELPING ME PUT UP THIS SWING.
WATTERSON
WHERE DID YOU EVER FIND THIS GREAT TIRE?
CALVIN! I'VE GOT TO GO TO WORK!!

WHAT'S THAT CEREAL YOU'RE EATING?
IT'S MY NEW FAVORITE, "CHOCOLATE FROSTED SUGAR BOMBS."
WATTERSON
HAVE A TASTE.
THANK YOU.
MFFPBTH!! S-SW-SW SWEET!!
ACTUALLY, THEY'RE KINDA BLAND TILL YOU SCOOP SUGAR ON 'EM.

Calvin and Hobbes
by WATTERSON
HOW COME WE PLAY WAR AND NOT PEACE?
TOO FEW ROLE MODELS.
I'LL BE THE FEARLESS AMERICAN DEFENDER OF LIBERTY AND DEMOCRACY..
... AND YOU CAN BE THE LOATHSOME GODLESS COMMUNIST OPPRESSOR.
WE'RE AT WAR, SO IF YOU GET HIT WITH A DART, YOU'RE DEAD AND THE OTHER SIDE WINS, OK?
GOTCHA.
GO!
WAP
WAP
WATTERSON
KIND OF A STUPID GAME, ISN'T IT?

CAN I BE EXCUSED?
NOT UNTIL YOU FINISH YOUR SALMON.
BLAUGHHH!
CAN I EAT IT UPSTAIRS WHILE I DO MY HOMEWORK?
WELL, I SUPPOSE.
WATTERSON
I BROUGHT YOU YOUR FAVORITE! HOW'S IT COMING?
WELL, I COULDN'T FIGURE OUT THIS SUBTRACTION PROBLEM, SO I PUT "ATLANTA, GEORGIA"...

HEY, SUSIE, WANNA SEE A MAGIC TRICK?
FIRST, I'LL NEED AN ORDINARY QUARTER...
!
NOW I'LL DISAPPEAR! HA HA HA!
HEY! DIDN'T I SAY IT WAS A TRICK??
WATTERSON

LOOK! A DECODER RING!
MILK
WOW! WE CAN SEND EACH OTHER SECRET MESSAGES IN CODE!
WATTERSON
HA HA! NOW MOM AND DAD WON'T BE ABLE TO UNDERSTAND US AT ALL!
...NOT THAT THEY DO ANYWAY...
MILK

RISE AND SHINE, CALVIN!
MFGPBTHBBPT
THE EARLY BIRD GETS THE WORM!
BIG INCENTIVE.
WATTERSON

I'VE DECIDED WE SHOULD BE "COOLER" THAN WE ARE.
WE'RE NOT COOL?
SURE WE'RE COOL. BUT WE'RE NOT AS COOL AS WE COULD BE.
COOL PEOPLE WEAR DARK GLASSES!
WATTERSON
IT'S COOL TO BUMP INTO THINGS?
YOU DON'T MOVE, YOU JUST HANG AROUND.

HEY, DAD, WILL YOU BUY ME A FLAME THROWER?
OF COURSE NOT. DON'T BE SILLY.
WATTERSON
EVEN IF I DIDN'T USE IT IN THE HOUSE?

Calvin and Hobbes
by WATTERSON
DID YOU ASK YOUR MOM IF YOU COULD JUMP OFF THE ROOF?
QUESTIONS I KNOW THE ANSWERS TO I DON'T NEED TO ASK, RIGHT?
IS THIS BLANKET BIG ENOUGH?
PERFECT!
SEE, I'LL JUST GRAB ALL THE CORNERS AND MAKE A PARACHUTE!
YOU CAN WATCH AS I FLOAT TO THE GROUND, GENTLY AS A LEAF!
GERONIMO!!
CRUNCH
HIS MOM'S GOING TO HAVE A FIT ABOUT THOSE ROSE BUSHES.
WATTERSON

I TOLD YOU I'M NOT SICK! WHAT'S THAT? WILL IT HURT?
IT'S A TONGUE DEPRESSOR. IT WON'T HURT AT ALL.
WHAT'S *THAT*? WILL IT HURT?
IT'S A STETHOSCOPE. IT WON'T HURT AT ALL.
WHAT'S *THAT*? WILL IT HURT?
IT'S A CATTLE PROD. IT HURTS A LITTLE LESS THAN A BRANDING IRON.
LITTLE KIDS HAVE NO SENSE OF HUMOR.
WATTERSON

HEY, DOC, WHY ARE YOU RUBBING MY ARM WITH COTTON? ARE YOU GOING TO PUT A LEECH THERE?
ARE YOU GOING TO BLEED ME? YOU'RE NOT GOING TO AMPUTATE, ARE YOU? **ARE** YOU??
WHAT'S THAT? IS THAT A SHOT? ARE YOU GOING TO... **AAUGHH! IT WENT CLEAR THROUGH MY ARM!!** OW OW OW OW!!!
I'M DYING! I HOPE YOU'VE PAID YOUR MALPRACTICE INSURANCE, YOU QUACK!! **WHERE'S MY MOM???!**
WATTERSON

"SAFARI AL" HACKS HIS WAY THROUGH THE JUNGLE!
SUDDENLY, A GIANT GORILLA RIPS THROUGH THE FOLIAGE!
WATTERSON
CLEAN YOUR ROOM.
WHAT?
YOU HEARD ME. IT'S A JUNGLE IN HERE!

I DON'T THINK I'LL GO TO SCHOOL TODAY.
I THINK YOU WILL.
I THINK I WON'T.
WATTERSON
RATS.

SEEN ANY UFOs YET?
NOPE.
KEEP WATCHING THE MOON. ALIENS USUALLY TRY TO SNEAK UP FROM BEHIND IT.
WHAT ARE YOU DOING OUT HERE IN YOUR PAJAMAS? GET BACK IN BED!!
MOTHERS, ON THE OTHER HAND, SNEAK UP FROM BEHIND THE PACHYSANDRA PATCH.
WATTERSON

GOOD NIGHT, HOBBES.
GOOD NIGHT.
DO YOU BELIEVE IN GHOSTS?
WATTERSON

Calvin and HOBBES
by WATTERSON
WHAT DO YOU HAVE FOR LUNCH, SUSIE? MAYBE I'LL TRADE YOU.
IT'S BOLOGNA!
UGH! A CROSS SECTION OF A DACHSHUND. NO, THANKS.
I WONDER WHAT I HAVE FOR LUNCH TODAY.
IT'S LUNCH TIME! HA HA HA! I THINK I'LL HAVE THIS LITTLE KID!!
HELP! I'M BEING EATEN ALIVE BY MY OWN LUNCH! SOMEBODY GET ME A FORK!
HE'S GOT ME!!
AAARRRGGHH
WHAM
WHAM
WHAM
WHAM
HA! I KILLED IT WITH MY THERMOS! SEE? IT'S BLEEDING JELLY!
NO WONDER THIS SEAT WASN'T TAKEN.
WATTERSON

SOMEWHERE IN COMMUNIST RUSSIA I'LL BET THERE'S A LITTLE BOY WHO HAS NEVER KNOWN ANYTHING BUT **CENSORSHIP** AND **OPPRESSION**.
BUT MAYBE HE'S HEARD ABOUT **AMERICA**, AND HE DREAMS OF LIVING IN THIS LAND OF **FREEDOM** AND OPPORTUNITY!
WATTERSON
SOMEDAY, I'D LIKE TO MEET THAT LITTLE BOY...
...AND TELL HIM THE AWFUL **TRUTH** ABOUT THIS PLACE!!
CALVIN, BE QUIET AND EAT THE STUPID LIMA BEANS.

WHENEVER I TAKE MY BATH...
...I ALWAYS PUT MY DUCKY IN FIRST.
WATTERSON
FOR COMPANIONSHIP?
TO TEST FOR SHARKS.

MY SECRET ANCIENT TREASURE MAP SAYS TO DIG HERE!
LOOK! A WALLET FULL OF MONEY! RIGHT WHERE YOU SAID!
IT'S DAD'S. I BURIED IT HERE LAST WEEK.
WATTERSON

SPACEMAN SPIFF, BOLD INTERPLANETARY EXPLORER, SPIES A ZARG!
SPIFF CALIBRATES HIS BLASTER. READY...AIM...
CALVIN, IF YOU SHOOT THAT PAPER CLIP AT ME, I'LL GET YOUR BOTTOM HAULED TO THE PRINCIPAL'S OFFICE SO FAST YOU'LL THINK YOU WERE IN A **TIME WARP**!!
CONFOUND IT. THE BLASTER JAMMED.
WATTERSON

IT LOOKS LIKE HOBBES BURST A SEAM HERE. I'LL GET MY SEWING KIT.
WATTERSON
IT'S JUST A LITTLE CUT. I DON'T NEED AN OPERATION. THIS IS UNNECESSARY SURGERY!
IT'S NOT SURGERY. YOU'RE JUST GETTING A COUPLE STITCHES! WHAT'S THE BIG DEAL?
YOUR MOM NEVER USES ANY ANESTHETIC.

WHAT A PECULIAR DREAM I HAD LAST NIGHT!
I DREAMED I WAS IN A BIG FIGHT WITH A FEROCIOUS WEASEL!
WHAT DO YOU SUPPOSE IT MEANS?
WATTERSON
IT MEANS YOU'RE SLEEPING ON THE FLOOR TONIGHT, YOU NINCOMPOOP!

Calvin and Hobbes
by WATTERSON
WHY SURE.
HEY DAD, REMEMBER OUR CAR?
WAIT A MINUTE. WHAT DO YOU MEAN, "REMEMBER"?
HOBBES, I HAVE A CONJECTURAL MORAL QUESTION. MAYBE YOU CAN HELP.
SURE.
SUPPOSE I DID SOMETHING BAD. SHOULD I TELL DAD?
HOW BAD ARE WE SUPPOSING?
WELL, HYPOTHETICALLY, LET'S SAY PRETTY BAD. LIKE TO HIS CAR, HYPOTHETICALLY.
HOW BAD, HYPOTHETICALLY, TO HIS CAR?
WELL, LET'S PRETEND IT WAS **REAL** BAD.
SHOULD WE PRETEND IT COULD BE FIXED?
IF WE IMAGINED HE COULD **FIND** THE CAR, WE COULD PRETEND IT MIGHT BE FIXED.
I SEE.
YOU CAN KEEP THE BOOK. I'LL CALL THE BUS STATION.
"¿QUE PASA, SEÑORITA? ¡I AM EL FUGITIVO!"
WATTERSON

WHY CAN'T I STAY UP LATE? YOU GUYS CAN!
IT'S NOT FAIR!
THE WORLD ISN'T FAIR, CALVIN.
I KNOW, BUT WHY ISN'T IT EVER UNFAIR IN MY FAVOR?
WATTERSON

THE VALIANT SPACEMAN SPIFF IS BEING PURSUED BY A DISGUSTING SCUM BEING!
SPIFF SPOTS HIS HOVERING SPACESHIP AND BOLTS FOR THE LADDER!
WATTERSON
BUT HE'S TOO LATE! THE AWFUL SCUM BEING IS UPON HIM! IT'S ALL OVER!
IT'S ALL OVER!!
I TOLD YOU THREE TIMES RECESS WAS OVER! NOW GET INSIDE!

AS DICTATOR, I HAVE THE SOLE VOICE IN GOVERNMENT!
I WILL NOT TOLERATE DISSENT!
I ALONE SHALL DECIDE THE GOOD! I ALONE SHALL..
TIME FOR BED, CALVIN.
COULDN'T WE VOTE ON THIS?
WATTERSON

IF YOU COULD WISH FOR ANYTHING, WHAT WOULD IT BE?
A BIG SUNNY FIELD TO BE IN.
A STUPID FIELD?! YOU'VE GOT THAT NOW! THINK BIG! RICHES! POWER! PRETEND YOU COULD HAVE ANYTHING!
WATTERSON
ACTUALLY, IT'S HARD TO ARGUE WITH SOMEONE WHO LOOKS SO HAPPY.
Z

HERE FISH!
WATTERSON
THEY MUST KNOW THAT ONE.

AAGHH!
CHOMP!
WATTERSON
ARE THE FISH BITING?
DROP DEAD, HOBBES.

Calvin and HobbEs
by WATTERSON
OOPS! I FORGOT TO READ CHAPTER FIVE FOR SCHOOL TOMORROW.
WHAT ARE YOU GOING TO DO?
CATCH A QUICK COLD.
COUGH COUGH
YOU SOUND TERRIBLE, CALVIN. I'LL GET YOU SOME COUGH MEDICINE.
IT WASN'T ME COUGHING. IT WAS HOBBES.
ME? IT WASN'T ME!
I KNOW, BUT THAT COUGH SYRUP TASTES AWFUL.
SO YOU'RE GOING TO HAVE ME TAKE IT? NOTHING DOING, BUSTER. I REFUSE!
HERE YOU GO, CALVIN. OPEN UP.
NOT ME! GIVE IT TO HOBBES! HE'S THE ONE WHO..
GLOOMP
ACKTHP!
PBTHBBPPTH!!
HACK
HACK
MMMM! THAT COUGH MEDICINE IS GOOD! YOU SHOULD TRY SOME! REALLY!
YOU'RE NOT FOOLING ME ONE BIT, YOU STINKER.
WATTERSON

I CAN'T GET THIS MODEL AIRPLANE TO LOOK RIGHT.
THESE DIRECTIONS ARE IMPOSSIBLE!
RRRRRGGGHHHHH
WHAM
WHAM
WHAM
HIT BY ANTI-AIRCRAFT GUNS.
YOUR PLANES DO SEEM TO RUN INTO THOSE, DON'T THEY?
WATTERSON

TOMMY TOLD A FUNNY STORY AT SCHOOL TODAY. I ALMOST DIED!
TELL IT TO ME.
WELL, ACTUALLY THE STORY ITSELF WASN'T SO FUNNY...
...IT WAS THE WAY HE TOLD IT.
HOW DID HE TELL IT?
HE WAS DRINKING MILK AND WHEN HE LAUGHED, IT CAME UP HIS NOSE!
WATTERSON

You've got two periods to live, Twinky.
Then it's gym class, and I turn you into hamburger casserole!
I HATE GYM CLASS.
COACH THINKS VIOLENCE IS AEROBIC.
WATTERSON

WHERE'S MY JACKET?
I'VE LOOKED EVERYWHERE! UNDER THE BED, OVER MY CHAIR...
...ON THE STAIRS, ON THE HALL FLOOR, IN THE KITCHEN... IT'S JUST NOT ANYWHERE!
OH, HERE IT IS! WHO PUT IT IN THE STUPID CLOSET?!?
WATTERSON

HOCUS-POCUS, ABRACADABRA!
I COMMAND MY HOMEWORK TO DO ITSELF! HOMEWORK, BE DONE!
WATTERSON
FLIP FLIP FLIP
RATS.

DO YOU EVER THINK ABOUT THE END OF THE WORLD AS WE KNOW IT?
YOU MEAN A NUCLEAR WAR?
WATTERSON
I THINK MOM WAS REFERRING TO IF SHE EVER CATCHES ME LETTING THE AIR OUT OF THE CAR TIRES AGAIN.

Calvin and Hobbes
by WATTERSON
WELL, THAT'S SHOWING A LITTLE FORESIGHT FOR ONCE. GOOD FOR YOU.
I'M TAKING THE UMBRELLA OUTSIDE.
WAIT A MINUTE...
YOU REALLY THINK THIS WILL WORK?
OF COURSE! LET'S GO!
SMASH!
BONK
BONK
BONK
WATTERSON
ITY BIPPITY BIPPITY BIPPITY
LOOK! I'M FLYING!!
I HAD MY EYES SHUT. HOW WAS IT?
GREAT! WHAT A RIDE! LET'S GET SOME OTHER KIDS AND CHARGE 'EM!

FEARLESS SPACEMAN SPIFF CLOSES IN ON THE FLEEING ZARGONS!
ONCE AGAIN OUR HERO IS ABOUT TO TEACH VICIOUS ALIEN SCUM THAT VIRTUE IS ITS OWN REWARD! HE LOCKS ONTO TARGET!
PSST, CALVIN! WHAT WAS THE CAPITAL OF POLAND UNTIL 1600?
KRAKOW.
THANKS.
KRAKOW! KRAKOW! TWO DIRECT HITS!
WATTERSON

THE TYRANNOSAURUS LUMBERS ACROSS THE PREHISTORIC VALLEY...
THE TERRIFYING LIZARD IS THREE STORIES TALL AND HIS MOUTH IS FILLED WITH SIX-INCH CHISELS OF DEATH!
WITH A FEW MIGHTY STEPS, THE DINOSAUR IS UPON A TRIBE OF FLEEING CAVEMEN. HE DEVOURS THEM ONE BY ONE!
AARRGH! AAIEEE! AAUGHH!
CALVIN, EAT YOUR POPCORN QUIETLY!
WATTERSON

WHAT DOES THIS WORD MEAN?
WHICH ONE?
THAT LONG ONE.
!
WATTERSON
I DON'T KNOW.
YOU DO TOO!! ALL RIGHT! WHERE'S A DICTIONARY??

CAN I WATCH THE MOVIE "KILLER PROM QUEEN" ON TV?
NO.
DO I HAVE TO EAT THIS SLIMY ASPARAGUS?
YES.
CAN I STAY UP TILL MIDNIGHT?
NO.
THERE'S AN INVERSE RELATIONSHIP BETWEEN HOW GOOD SOMETHING IS FOR YOU, AND HOW MUCH FUN IT IS.
WATTERSON

LET'S SEE WHAT HAPPENS IF YOU COOK POPCORN WITHOUT A LID.
POW
KAPWING
POW
BANG
ZANG
BOING
HECK, THAT'S MORE FUN THAN EXPLODING A POTATO IN THE MICROWAVE!
LET'S DO SOME MORE!
WATTERSON

C'MON, CALVIN. WE'RE GOING TO THE STORE.
CAN HOBBES COME?
NO, JUST LEAVE HIM HERE.
BUT I WANT HIM TO COME WITH US!!
IF YOU CAN'T WIN BY REASON, GO FOR VOLUME.
WATTERSON

Calvin and HOBBES
by WATTERSON
HONEY, WE HAVE TO LEAVE SOON. IS CALVIN TAKING HIS BATH?
OH GOOD.
WHILE I'M TAKING MY BATH, YOU CAN BRUSH YOUR TEETH AND COMB YOUR HAIR.
RIGHT.
YOUR DAD WON'T MIND IF I USE HIS COLOGNE, WILL HE?
WELL, GO EASY THIS TIME.
THINK I SHOULD SHAVE?
NO, GO FOR THE DON JOHNSON FUZZY LOOK.
HERE'S A TIE AND ONE OF MY SPORT COATS.
PERFECT! RIGHT OUT OF "GQ"!
BOY, I LOOK GOOD IN ANYTHING, DON'T I?
REFRESH MY MEMORY. HOW DID I GET TALKED INTO THIS ONE?
MY FRIEND WOULD LIKE TO SEE THE WINE LIST.
Menu
WATTERSON

SO THE CONTRACTOR SAYS IT WILL COST ABOUT $200 TO FIX.
OH, THAT DUMB KID!
WELL, IT'S ALL PART OF RAISING A CHILD, RIGHT?
MM.
YOU'RE NOT SORRY WE HAD CALVIN, ARE YOU?
ARE **YOU**?
WATTERSON
I ASKED FIRST.... BESIDES, IT WASN'T ALL **MY** DECISION.
ALL **I** KNOW IS THAT **I** OFFERED TO BUY US A DACHSHUND, BUT NO, **YOU** SAID...

DO YOU THINK THERE'S A GOD?
WELL **SOME**BODY'S OUT TO GET ME.
WATTERSON

SPACEMAN SPIFF CLOSES IN ON THE ALIEN VESSEL!
THE ALIEN, BEING UNNATURALLY STUPID, IS BLISSFULLY IGNORANT OF ITS IMMINENT DOOM!
OUR HERO LOCKS ONTO TARGET AND WARMS UP HIS FRAP-RAY BLASTER!
WATTERSON
MISS WORMWOOD!!
ZOUNDS! A GORKON DEATH STATION APPEARS! EVASIVE ACTION!

WHACK!
WATTERSON
WOW! ANOTHER HOLE IN ONE!

WOW! THREE NEW MAGAZINES FOR ME TODAY.
YESTERDAY I GOT FIVE. I LOVE GETTING ALL THIS MAIL.
HOW COME YOU RECEIVE ALL THESE MAGAZINES?
WATTERSON
I WENT TO THE LIBRARY AND FILLED OUT ALL THE SUBSCRIPTION CARDS THAT SAID "BILL ME LATER."

I LOVE SATURDAY MORNING CARTOONS.
WHAT CLASSIC HUMOR!
THIS IS WHAT ENTERTAINMENT IS ALL ABOUT.
WATTERSON
...IDIOTS, EXPLOSIVES, AND FALLING ANVILS.

Calvin and HOBBES
by WATTERSON
WANNA GO CATCH SOME FISH?
SURE.
UGH. I DON'T WANT TO TOUCH THESE WORMS. WILL YOU PUT ONE ON MY HOOK?
ME? I'M NOT GONNA SPEAR ANY WORMS!
I KNOW... LET'S JUST DUMP THE WORMS IN THE WATER, AND WHEN THE FISH COME UP TO EAT THEM, WE'LL CATCH THEM IN THE NET!
PRETTY SMART, HUH? THAT'S WHAT I LIKE ABOUT SURVIVING IN THE WILD – PITTING OUR WITS AGAINST THE RAGING ELEMENTS!
THE WORMS ARE GETTING SOGGY.
OOH, THEY'RE STARTING TO SINK.
BLIP
BLOOP
BLORP
LET'S PIT OUR WITS AGAINST SOME FAST FOOD CHEESEBURGERS. THOSE COME IN NEAT LITTLE BOXES.
YEAH, WHO'D WANT TO EAT SOMETHING THAT EATS WORMS ANYWAY?
WATTERSON

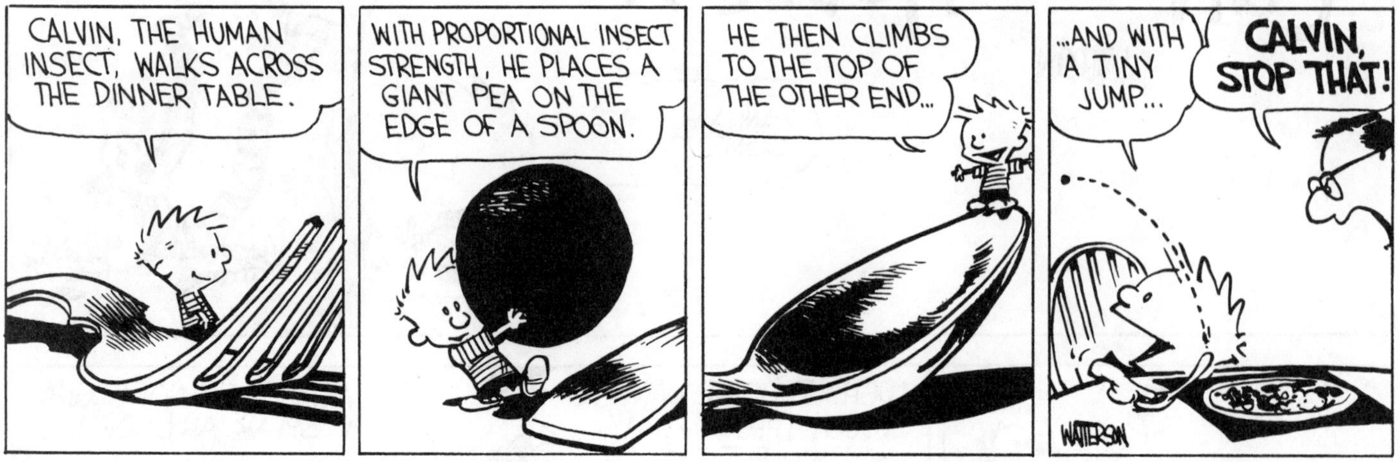
CALVIN, THE HUMAN INSECT, WALKS ACROSS THE DINNER TABLE.
WITH PROPORTIONAL INSECT STRENGTH, HE PLACES A GIANT PEA ON THE EDGE OF A SPOON.
HE THEN CLIMBS TO THE TOP OF THE OTHER END...
...AND WITH A TINY JUMP...
CALVIN, STOP THAT!

IN HIS MINUSCULE SIZE, IT TAKES CALVIN, THE HUMAN INSECT, TEN MINUTES TO WALK ACROSS A BOOK'S PAGE!
AT THE OTHER END, HE SLOWLY LIFTS THE GIGANTIC SHEET!
95
THEN IT'S ANOTHER TEN-MINUTE JOURNEY BACK, AS HE TURNS IT OVER!
GEE, THE KID'S BEEN QUIET FOR ALMOST TWENTY MINUTES.
HE'S DOING HIS HOMEWORK.

HERE'S A MOVIE WE SHOULD WATCH.
WHO'S IN IT?
IT SAYS, "JAPANESE CAST."
"TWO BIG RUBBERY MONSTERS SLUG IT OUT OVER MAJOR METROPOLITAN CENTERS IN A BATTLE FOR WORLD SUPREMACY."
DOESN'T THAT SOUND GREAT?
AND PEOPLE SAY THAT FOREIGN FILM IS INACCESSIBLE.

OH, ROSALYN, YOU'RE HERE! GOOD, COME IN!
WE REALLY APPRECIATE YOUR COMING ON SUCH SHORT NOTICE. WE'VE HAD A TERRIBLE TIME GETTING A BABY SITTER FOR TONIGHT.
HA HA. MAYBE LITTLE CALVIN HERE HAS GOTTEN HIMSELF A REPUTATION.
WATTERSON
HA HA. YOU HAVE THE HALF UP FRONT?
YES, LET ME GET MY PURSE...

HI, BABY DOLL, IT'S ME. YEAH, I'M BABY SITTING THE KID DOWN THE STREET.
YEAH, THAT'S RIGHT, THE LITTLE MONSTER. ...HMM?... WELL SO FAR, NO PROBLEM.
WATTERSON
HE HASN'T BEEN ANY TROUBLE. YOU JUST HAVE TO SHOW THESE KIDS WHO'S THE BOSS. ..MM HMM..
HOW MUCH LONGER TILL SHE LETS US OUT OF THE GARAGE?
SHE SAID 8 O'CLOCK, AND IT'S ALMOST 6:30 NOW...

THANKS AGAIN FOR BABY SITTING, ROSALYN.
CALVIN WAS NO TROUBLE AT ALL.
THAT'S GOOD. I'LL GET THE CAR AND DRIVE YOU HOME.
THERE YOU GO. GOOD NIGHT.
THANK YOU. GOOD NIGHT.
IS SHE GONE?
WATTERSON

Calvin and HOBBES by WATTERSON
WE'VE GOT A BABY SITTER TONIGHT.
READY?
READY.
CALVIN, THE BABY SITTER IS HERE! WE'RE GOING! BE GOOD, OK?
HI THERE. YOU MUST BE CALVIN.
HMMPH.
YOU'RE NOT MY MOM, SO I DON'T HAVE TO DO ANYTHING YOU SAY. I'M GOING TO DO WHATEVER I FEEL LIKE, SO JUST STAY OUT OF THE WAY.
CALVIN, TAKE A LOOK BY THE TELEPHONE AND TELL ME WHAT YOU SEE.
A NOTE MOM LEFT WITH EMERGENCY NUMBERS
RIGHT. NOW YOU WOULDN'T WANT ME TO HAVE TO CALL ANY OF THOSE NUMBERS, WOULD YOU?
WATTERSON
WELL, IT MUST BE 6:30. GUESS I'LL TURN IN.
FOR EIGHT BUCKS A NIGHT, I DON'T PUT UP WITH MUCH.

WHAT A GREAT NIGHT TO CAMP OUT!
WHERE'S OUR TENT? I THOUGHT THE SCOUTMASTER SAID TO SET THEM UP.
UH OH.
WHEN HE SAID TO PITCH THE TENT, I THREW IT AWAY.
WATTERSON

THE BEST PART ABOUT THESE HIKES IS GETTING TO SEE SO MUCH WILDLIFE.
LOOK! A TIGER!
A TIGER?!
DON'T DO THAT!
WATTERSON

WE'RE SEPARATED FROM THE TROOP AND HOPELESSLY LOST!
LEFT ALONE IN THE UNCOMPROMISING WILD TO SURVIVE BY OUR WITS UNAIDED!
HEY, DUMMY! THE SCOUTMASTER SAYS TO GRAB YOUR STUPID STUFFED TIGER AND GET YOUR REAR IN GEAR!
WATTERSON
WE'LL TRY TO LOSE 'EM AGAIN OVER THE NEXT HILL.

GRAB THE HOTDOGS AND COME ON!
THE TROOP'S COOKING DINNER OVER THE FIRE.
OH THAT'S JUST GREAT.
HERE WE'VE BEEN LUGGING THIS DUMB MICROWAVE AROUND FOR NOTHING.
WATTERSON

BOP
SPIKE!
WATTERSON
OH OH, WE'D BETTER LEAVE!
IT LOOKS LIKE SOME BIG PEOPLE WANT TO PLAY TENNIS.

THE CROCODILE FLOATS TO THE TOP OF THE MURKY AMAZON...
COMPLETELY MOTIONLESS, HE APPEARS TO BE ONLY A HARMLESS LOG.
A HIPPOPOTAMUS APPROACHES AND ENSURES ITS INSTANT DEATH!
WATTERSON
CALVIN, WHAT ARE YOU DOING? ARE YOU ALL RIGHT?
CLOSER... CLOSER...

Calvin and HOBBES
by WATTERSON
LOOK, IT SAYS YOU HAVE TO BE EIGHTEEN TO BUY CIGARETTES.
EIGHTEEN?!? BY THEN I'LL KNOW BETTER!
MOM, CAN I HAVE A CIGARETTE?
SURE, CALVIN. I THINK YOUR GRANDFATHER LEFT SOME HERE. JUST SMOKE OUTSIDE, OK?
WOW!
YOUR MOM LET YOU HAVE A CIGARETTE?
FOR A MOM, SOMETIMES SHE'S PRETTY COOL.
EEEEEEP
BLAAUGH!
GAG
HACK
COUGH
YOU'D THINK THIS WOULD BE AN EASY HABIT TO BREAK.
WHEEZE
ACK
WATTERSON
WELL NOW... DID WE LEARN A LITTLE LESSON TODAY?
GASP ..YES...
TRUSTING PARENTS CAN BE HAZARDOUS TO YOUR HEALTH.

MOM! MOM! A BIG DOG KNOCKED ME DOWN AND HE STOLE HOBBES!
I TRIED TO CATCH HIM, BUT I COULDN'T, AND NOW I'VE LOST MY BEST FRIEND!
WELL CALVIN, IF YOU WOULDN'T DRAG THAT TIGER EVERYWHERE, THINGS LIKE THIS WOULDN'T HAPPEN.
THERE'S NO PROBLEM SO AWFUL THAT YOU CAN'T ADD SOME GUILT TO IT AND MAKE IT EVEN WORSE!
WATTERSON

I CAN'T SLEEP AT ALL. POOR HOBBES! I WONDER WHERE HE IS. I HOPE HE'S OK.
SNIFF.. WHAT DID I EVER DO TO DESERVE THIS?
WHATEVER IT WAS, I'M *SORRY* ALREADY!
WATTERSON

Lost: My tiGER, "HobbEs"
MAYBE YOU SHOULD DESCRIBE HIM.
ON tHE QUIEt sidE. SOMEwhat PECuliar. A Good Companion, in a WEird Sort of way.
I MEAN, WHAT DOES HE LOOK LIKE?
OH.
WATTERSON

WELL LOOK, SOMEBODY LEFT A STUFFED TIGER OUT IN THE FIELD. HOW STRANGE.
LOOKS LIKE A DOG'S BEEN CHEWING ON YOU, FELLA.
WELL, NOTHING A LITTLE TEA PARTY WITH SOME OTHER STUFFED ANIMALS WOULDN'T HELP. C'MON.
WATTERSON

HOBBES! HOBBES! WHERE ARE YOU ?!?
HELLO, CALVIN. WOULD YOU LIKE TO JOIN MY TEA PARTY?
HECK NO. I'M TRYING TO FIND MY BEST FRIEND, WHO'S BEEN KIDNAPPED BY A DOG. LEAVE ME ALONE.
WELL I THINK MR. CALVIN IS VERY RUDE, DON'T YOU, MR. TIGER? YES, I THINK SO TOO. MORE TEA, ANYONE?
WATTERSON

HEY, I SHOULD TELL SUSIE TO KEEP HER EYES OPEN FOR HOBBES.
SUSIE, I...
HOBBES!
YOU FOUND HOBBES! THANK YOU THANK YOU THANKYOUTHANKYOUTHANKYOUTHANKYOUTHANKYOUTHA
WATTERSON
WELL! WASN'T MR. CALVIN A GENTLEMAN! I DO HOPE... HEY! WHO TOOK ALL THE COOKIES?!?

Calvin and Hobbes by WATTERSON
WHAT'S THAT SMELL?
EITHER MOM'S COOKING DINNER, OR SOMEBODY GOT SICK IN THE FURNACE DUCT.
BOY, DOES IT STINK IN HERE! WHAT ARE YOU COOKING FOR DINNER?!
WHATEVER IT IS, I'M NOT EATING IT.
I'M STEWING SOME MONKEY HEADS.
MONKEY HEADS?
THEY'LL BE SOGGY ENOUGH TO EAT IN ABOUT TWENTY MINUTES.
WATTERSON
REALLY?? WE'RE HAVING MONKEY HEADS? WE ARE NOT. ...ARE THOSE REALLY MONKEY HEADS?
I'VE NEVER HAD MONKEY HEADS BEFORE! I WONDER WHAT THEY'RE LIKE.
WOW! MONKEY HEADS!
MM...KINDA SQUISHY. OOH LOOK, IS THAT A NOSE? WHAT'S THIS? BRAINS? I DIDN'T THINK THEY'D BE SO RUBBERY...
WHAT? I THOUGHT THESE WERE STUFFED PEPPERS. HONEY, WHAT THE HECK IS THIS?? WHATEVER IT IS, I'M NOT EATING IT!

SUSIE, WANNA HEAR A SECRET?
SURE.
I THINK THE PRINCIPAL IS A SPACE ALIEN SPY.
HE'S TRYING TO CORRUPT OUR YOUNG INNOCENT MINDS SO WE'LL BE UNABLE TO RESIST WHEN HIS PEOPLE INVADE EARTH!
PROMISE NOT TO TELL ANYONE?
DON'T WORRY.
WATTERSON

HOBBES, WHAT SHOULD I DO WHEN MOE COMES TO BEAT ME UP IN GYM CLASS?
WELL, YOU CAN ALWAYS DO WHAT WE TIGERS DO WHEN A RHINO CHARGES.
WATTERSON
WHAT'S THAT?
WE SCRAMBLE LIKE MANIACS FOR THE NEAREST TREE.
THAT'S YOUR ADVICE?? TO SIT IN A TREE ALL DAY?!?
IT DOESN'T IMPRESS THE GIRLS, OF COURSE, BUT THERE'S NO SENSE IMPRESSING THEM AND THEN GETTING KILLED, MY DAD USED TO SAY...

HOBBES, I NEED YOUR HELP. THAT BULLY MOE KEEPS PUSHING ME AROUND.
...SO I WANT YOU TO COME TO SCHOOL AND EAT HIM, OK?
WATTERSON
EAT HIM?
SURE! TIGERS EAT PEOPLE ALL THE TIME!
WHAT IF THE CAFETERIA LADIES WON'T LET ME USE THE OVEN?

IT'S TOO EARLY TO BE IN BED. IT'S HARDLY EVEN DARK OUT. WHY DO I HAVE TO BE IN BED? IT'S RIDICULOUS.
I'M NOT EVEN TIRED! I DON'T NEED TO BE IN BED! THIS IS AN OUTRAGE!
IT'S THE STUPIDEST THING I CAN IMAGINE! I THINK MOM AND DAD ARE JUST TRYING TO GET RID OF ME. I CAN'T SLEEP AT ALL. CAN YOU SLEEP, HOBBES?
NO!

OK, MOM, HOBBES AND I HAVE FORMED A LOBBY. WE WANT MORE PRIVILEGES!
MORE PRIVILEGES? LIKE WHAT? YOU'VE GOT IT MADE!
NO RESPONSIBILITIES, NO CARES, NO WORRIES! WHAT MORE COULD YOU POSSIBLY WANT?
WHY DIDN'T YOU TELL HER ABOUT THE CREDIT CARDS IN OUR NAMES?
YOU HEARD HER. SHE'S IN ONE OF HER MOODS.

I LOVE SATURDAYS!
EVERY SATURDAY I GET UP AT SIX AND EAT THREE BOWLS OF CRUNCHY SUGAR BOMBS.
THEN I WATCH CARTOONS TILL NOON, AND I'M INCOHERENT AND HYPERACTIVE THE REST OF THE DAY.
DOES IT WORK?
NO BROTHERS OR SISTERS **SO** FAR!

Calvin and Hobbes
by WATTERSON
NO EARTHLING HAS EVER BEFORE SEEN THE CRATERED, SCARRED SURFACE OF DISTANT PLANET ZOG!
... ALTHOUGH IT'S NOT UNLIKE SOME OF THOSE ZIT CREAM COMMERCIALS...
WE JOIN THE FEARLESS SPACEMAN SPIFF, INTERPLANETARY EXPLORER EXTRAORDINAIRE, OUT AT THE FARTHEST REACHES OF THE GALAXY...
WITH NERVES OF STEEL, OUR HERO SETS FORTH ON HIS DANGEROUS MISSION!
HE FIRES HIS HYPER-JETS AND...
...BLASTS INTO THE FIFTH DIMENSION!
INTO A WORLD BEYOND HUMAN COMPREHENSION!
INTO A WORLD WHERE TIME HAS NO MEANING!
WATTERSON
MAN, THIS CLASS LASTS FOREVER!
SO WE CARRY THE THREE INTO THE TENS COLUMN ....

IN THE COMMERCIALS, THIS COLA GREATLY INCREASES ONE'S SEX APPEAL.
GLIK GLIK GLICK GLICK
BUR-UR-URPP!!
EVIDENTLY A LITTLE LICENSE ON MADISON AVENUE'S PART.
PHOO! RIGHT UP MY NOSE.
WATTERSON

IT'S AN OUTRAGE THAT SIX-YEAR-OLDS CAN'T VOTE!
HERE I AM, A U.S. CITIZEN, WITH NO VOICE IN OUR REPRESENTATIVE GOVERNMENT!
YOU'RE CONCERNED ABOUT THE DIRECTION THE COUNTRY IS HEADED?
NO, I JUST WANT A BIGGER PIECE OF THE PIE.
WATTERSON

POOF POOF POOF
POW!
GOOD HEAVENS, I THINK I BLEW MY FACE INSIDE OUT!
WATTERSON

THE WATER'S TOO COLD!
NOW IT'S TOO HOT.
NOW IT'S TOO COLD.
WATTERSON
NOW IT'S TOO DEEP.

THE FEARSOME SHARK SENSES DISTRESS IN THE WAVES ABOVE HIM!
HE CIRCLES UP, CLOSER AND CLOSER TO THE TERRIFIED VICTIM!
HEY!
YAHH!
SNAP
THRASH
SNAP
WATTERSON
YOU KNOW, FOR SOMEONE WHO HATES BATHS AS MUCH AS YOU DO, YOU'RE NOT MAKING THIS GO ANY FASTER!
ANOTHER GRUESOME KILL...

HERE, CALVIN, I'LL SHOW YOU A MAGIC TRICK.
SEE? I PULLED A DIME FROM YOUR EAR! PRETTY GOOD, HUH?
ANYTHING YET?
J-JUST A B-B-BLOODY N-NOSE.
WATTERSON

Calvin and Hobbes
by WATTERSON
WE SHOULD MAKE DAD A FATHER'S DAY CARD.
OKAY, I'LL DRAW A PICTURE OF HIM ON IT.
HMM... MAKE HIS MOUTH BIGGER. HE USUALLY LOOKS ANGRIER THAN THAT.
GOOD MORNING, DAD! HAPPY FATHER'S DAY!
MMF. GOOMRG.
IN APPRECIATION OF YOUR SERVICE AS DAD, TODAY I AM LIVING ACCORDING TO THE PRINCIPLES OF YOUR FATHERLY WISDOM.
CALVIN, WHAT TIME IS... FIVE IN THE MORNING?!
YES, "EARLY TO BED, EARLY TO RISE," YOU ALWAYS SAY...
I WAS GOING TO BUY YOU A NICE PRESENT, BUT "A PENNY SAVED IS A PENNY EARNED," AS YOU SAY...
..SO I'M NOW EARNING 6% ON THE MONEY I DIDN'T SPEND.
YES, DAD, THANKS TO YOU, I'M A HAPPIER, BETTER PERSON.
GOOD WORK, SOCRATES.
I KNEW WE'D MADE A MISTAKE THE MINUTE I SAW THAT LITTLE BOLOGNA LOAF IN THE HOSPITAL BASSINET.
WATTERSON

I'VE NEVER BEEN THIS HIGH IN A TREE BEFORE.
ME EITHER. YOU CAN SEE FOR MILES FROM UP HERE.
WATTERSON
I'LL SAY! I'M GLAD WE'RE UP HERE.
THAT WAS QUITE A CRASH, WASN'T IT?

THE RAIN STOPPED!
THIS IS THE BEST TIME TO GO WORMUCKING. LET'S GO!
WATTERSON
WHAT'S THAT?
IT'S WHEN YOU WALK ON THE PAVEMENT AND MUCK ALL THE WORMS.

CALVIN, QUIT CHARGING AROUND THE HOUSE!!
SMASH!
BINK
BONK
BOOM
WHAT DID I JUST TELL YOU?!?
WATTERSON
BEATS ME. WEREN'T YOU LISTENING EITHER?

BANG! YOU'RE DEAD!
NO I'M NOT. YOU MISSED!
WATTERSON
I DID NOT! YOU CHEATER!
I'M HERE TALKING TO YOU, AREN'T I?
OK, THEN.. BANG!
MY, WHAT A MISERABLE SHOT YOU ARE!

HURRY UP, CALVIN. OUR RESERVATION IS FOR 7:00.
CAN HOBBES COME TO THE RESTAURANT?
NO.
WHY NOT?
WE'RE AFRAID HE MIGHT EAT SOMEONE. LET'S GO.
THAT'S RIGHT. YOU PROBABLY *WOULD*, WOULDN'T YOU?
I CAN NEVER STAY ON A DIET IN A RESTAURANT.

ARR! LOOK ALIVE, YE SCURVY SCALLIWAGS! THAR'S A FRIGATE TO BOARD!
RUN UP THE SKULL AND CROSSBONES!
PREPARE THE PLANK!
WATTERSON
OUR SHIP **IS** A PLANK.
AND YOU'RE GOING TO WALK IT, WISE GUY!

Calvin and HOBBES
by WATTERSON
PTOO!
BLAT
WAP
THOK
BONK!
WATTERSON
POOM
WUNK
NICE DOUBLE PLAY. WHO'S OUT?
IT DEPENDS. ARE YOU ON *MY* TEAM, OR AM I ON *YOUR* TEAM?

A BEE LANDED ON YOUR BACK!
A BEE?! ACCKK! GET IT AWAY!!
DON'T MOVE, AND IT WON'T STING YOU.
JUST STAND STILL AND TRY NOT TO IMAGINE THAT IT MIGHT VERY WELL CRAWL DOWN YOUR SHIRT AND INTO YOUR PANTS!
YOWW!
HE IMAGINED IT.
WATTERSON

OK, LET'S FLUSH IT!
FLUSH
HA HA HA
HA
WHIZZZZ
HA
WATTERSON
HEE HEE! THAT WAS GREAT! LET'S DO IT AGAIN!
FLUSH
I DON'T WANT TO KNOW WHAT HE'S DOING. DO YOU?
NO. LET'S GO CHECK.

I'VE HAD TROUBLE CHOOSING A NEW HOBBY.
FIRST I WANTED TO COLLECT BUGS.
THEN I WANTED TO COLLECT STAMPS.
WHAT DID YOU DECIDE ON?
STAMPED BUGS.
WATTERSON

EVERYBODY I KNOW HAS EITHER CABLE TV OR A VCR! THEY CAN WATCH ANYTHING THEY WANT!
WATTERSON
BUT ME? I HAVE TO WATCH DUMB OL' SUMMER REPEATS! I HAVE TO WATCH THE SAME GARBAGE OVER AND OVER!
HOW CRUELLY WE MISTREAT YOU, CALVIN.
...SO THEN HE GAVE ME "OLIVER TWIST" TO READ, AND SAID I MIGHT IDENTIFY WITH IT.
RATS...AND "SORORITY ROW HORROR" IS ON CABLE TONIGHT.

I GOT A HELIUM BALLOON.
VERY NICE.
I'M GOING TO STAND ON THIS LADDER AND LET THE BALLOON CARRY ME UP AND AWAY.
NOTHING'S HAPPENING.
TRY JUMPING.
SEE? THERE GOES THE BALLOON. YOU DIDN'T HANG ON.
WATTERSON

WATTERSON
FLUSH!
WHEEE! HA HA HA!
I'M DONE WITH MY BATH.
MM... THAT WAS QUICK.

Calvin and HOBBES
by WATTERSON
CALVIN, QUIT HORSING AROUND!
HOBBES IS CROWDING ME.
THIS IS MY HALF OF THE SEAT, GOT IT, STRIPEYPANTS? THAT'S YOUR SIDE! YOU STAY OVER THERE!
I SEE THAT!!
CALVIN, I'M TRYING TO CONCENTRATE. BE QUIET.
HOBBES POKED ME.
I DON'T CARE WHAT HOBBES DID! JUST BE QUIET UNTIL WE GET OUT OF THIS TRAFFIC.
HEE HEE! (STOP IT. YOU HEARD DAD!)
GKKPT! PTHB!
HOO HOO! GKPTHB! (WE'RE GONNA GET IN TROUBLE!)
HEE HEE
WATTERSON
MMP MP! (SHHHH!) HEE HEE!
HEE HOO HA HEE
HA HA
HO HA
CALVIN! I THOUGHT I SAID I WANTED IT QUIET!!
WE WERE HAVING A WEIRD FACE CONTEST, DAD, BUT WE'RE ALL THROUGH NOW.
YOU WON.

WHAT'S ALL THE RUCKUS?! YOU'RE SUPPOSED TO BE ASLEEP!
AND WHAT'S WITH ALL THESE FEATHERS?! ARE YOU TEARING UP YOUR PILLOWS?!
IT WAS INCREDIBLE, DAD! A HERD OF DUCKS FLEW IN THE WINDOW AND MOLTED! THEY LEFT WHEN THEY HEARD YOU COMING! HONEST!
NICE ALIBI, FRIZZLETOP! NO DESSERT FOR A WEEK!
YOU WANT ANOTHER PILLOW ACROSS THE KISSER? I DIDN'T HEAR YOU OFFER ANY BRAINSTORMS!

YOU SEE, HOBBES, I HAVE A WATER BALLOON, AND YOU DON'T.
I THEREFORE HAVE OFFENSIVE SUPERIORITY, SO YOU HAVE TO DO WHAT I SAY. WHAT DO YOU THINK OF THAT?
I THINK I'LL TAKE THIS STICK AND POKE YOUR BALLOON.
THAT'S THE TROUBLE WITH WEAPONS TECHNOLOGY. IT BECOMES OBSOLETE SO QUICKLY.

OH MY GOSH, HOBBES! DON'T MOVE!
WHAT? WHAT IS IT?
THE BIGGEST, UGLIEST, FUZZIEST CATERPILLAR I'VE EVER SEEN IS ABOUT TO CHOMP YOUR BOTTOM!
AAUGH! KILL IT! KILL IT!
YOWW!
WHAM!
YOU KNOW WHAT YOUR PROBLEM IS? YOU'VE GOT NO APPRECIATION FOR PHYSICAL HUMOR, THAT'S WHAT!

WHERE ARE YOU GOING?
I'M GOING TO WALK TO THE OTHER SIDE OF THE LAKE.
WHAT'S THE BUCKET FOR?
TO DRAIN THE LAKE.
WATTERSON

YOU KNOW WHAT I LIKE ABOUT SUMMER DAYS?
THEY'RE JUST MADE FOR DOING THINGS.
...EVEN IF IT'S NOTHING.
ESPECIALLY IF IT'S NOTHING.
WATTERSON

THIS LOOKS LIKE A GREAT PLACE TO CATCH A CRAWDAD.
WHAT WILL WE DO WITH IT IF WE CATCH ONE?
WELL THAT'S ONE THING WE DON'T NEED TO WORRY ABOUT.
WATTERSON
YOU DON'T KNOW WHAT ONE IS EITHER, HUH?

Calvin and Hobbes
by WATTERSON
HOBBES, YOU DIDN'T BRING YOUR SWIM TRUNKS HERE TO THE BEACH!
NO, I PREFER "FURRY DIPPING."
YAAAAAYY!
OW OW OW HOT HOT HOT HOT
AAAAAAHHHHHHHH
SPLOOP
SPLOP
BBBRRRR! COLD COLD COLD
OW OW OW HOT HOT HOT HOT HOT
WATTERSON
DON'T TELL ME WE DROVE AN HOUR AND A HALF FOR THIS!

Calvin and HOBBES
by WATTERSON
GUESS WHAT'S SHORT AND UGLY AND WET ALL OVER! ...GIVE UP?
THE ANSWER HAD BETTER NOT BE WHAT I THINK IT IS...
SQUIRT SQUIRT SQUIRT SQUIRT SQUIRT SQUIRT SQUIRT
YOW!
SQUIRT SQUIRT SQUIRT
BANG BONK BING
CALVIN!
IF YOU'RE GOING TO TEAR AROUND, DO IT OUTSIDE!!
OKAY, OKAY...
WATTERSON

WHEN ARE WE GOING TO GET TO OUR VACATION SITE? I WANNA ***BE*** THERE!
CALVIN, IT'S AN EIGHT-HOUR DRIVE. WE'RE NOT EVEN OUT OF OUR STATE YET. IT'S GOING TO BE A WHILE. RELAX.
WATTERSON
HOW MUCH LONGER ***NOW***?
I TOLD YOU WE SHOULD HAVE FLOWN.

THERE'S A RESTAURANT COMING UP. WANT TO STOP?
ONLY IF THEY HAVE HAMBURGERS.
WATTERSON
HAMBURGERS? THAT'S ALL WE'VE EATEN THIS WHOLE STUPID TRIP! HAMBURGERS, HAMBURGERS, HAMBURGERS!
I'M SICK OF HAMBURGERS! WE'RE EATING SOMETHING ELSE FOR ONCE!
TEN MILLION BOTTLES OF BEER ON THE WALL, TEN MILLION BOTTLES OF BEER...
OK! OK! HERE'S A HAMBURGER JOINT! ***ARE YOU HAPPY?!***

I HAVE TO GO TO THE BATHROOM.
CALVIN, WE JUST PULLED OUT OF THE RESTAURANT. CAN'T YOU WAIT? THINK OF SOMETHING ELSE.
WATTERSON
ALL I CAN THINK OF IS NIAGARA FALLS, AND THE HOOVER DAM, AND NOAH'S ARK, AND...
OOH BOY, NOW ***I*** HAVE TO GO!
NEXT YEAR I SWEAR I'LL JUST TAKE A VACATION BY MYSELF.

THAT TRIP WAS EXCRUCIATING. THANK GOODNESS WE'RE HERE.
EIGHT HOURS CRAMMED IN A CAR WITH A HYPERACTIVE SIX-YEAR-OLD! WHAT AN ORDEAL!
WATTERSON
WELL, NOW CALVIN CAN RUN AND SCREAM ALL HE LIKES. AHH, WHAT A GREAT LITTLE PLACE.
I'M BORED. WHEN ARE WE LEAVING?
YOU'RE BORED? WOULD YOU LIKE ME TO SHOW YOU HOW AN ANCHOR WORKS?

AHH! ANOTHER GLORIOUS SUNRISE, AND NOT A SOUL AROUND!
THIS IS THE LIFE! A BRISK SWIM AT DAWN, A MORNING OUT IN A BOAT...
...AND BY 9 A.M., I'M BACK WITH FRESHLY CAUGHT FISH FOR BREAKFAST! THE DAY'S HARDLY BEGUN! WHAT A VACATION!
WATTERSON
UGH...I'VE SEEN CHEERIER FACES AT THE OFFICE!
YOU EAT YOUR DEAD ANIMALS. ALL I WANT IS SOME COFFEE.
WHY ISN'T THERE ANY TV UP HERE? I HATE THIS PLACE.

DAD, LOOK! I CAUGHT A FISH!
HEY, THAT'S A BIG ONE. I'LL SHOW YOU HOW TO CLEAN IT, AND WE'LL HAVE IT FOR DINNER.
"CLEAN IT"?
CUT OFF ITS HEAD AND GUT IT.
WATTERSON
MMM! PASS ME ANOTHER OF THESE GREAT CHEESE SANDWICHES! HA HA, NO BONES IN **THESE**, RIGHT?

WOW, LOOK DOWN THERE! I THINK THAT'S THE DIM OUTLINE OF A WHALE!
I THINK THAT'S A ROCK.
AND THAT MUST BE A GIANT EEL SLITHERING UP FROM THE BOTTOM!
I THINK THAT'S A WEED.
I'LL BET THIS IS THE MAST OF AN OLD SPANISH GALLEON, SUNK HUNDREDS OF YEARS AGO.
IT'S A BRANCH.
MAN, THIS IS BORING. I WISH THERE WAS A MOVIE THEATER SOMEPLACE.
WATTERSON

WANT TO GO FISHING?
SURE.
FISHING IS ONE SPORT I REALLY LIKE.
I CAN SEE WHY... IT'S SO CONTEMPLATIVE.
THERE'S ANOTHER ONE!!
WATTERSON

GZZZZZZZZZZZ
WAAAUUGHHH!
SPLOOSH
WATTERSON

WATTERSON
STOMP STOMP STOMP STOMP
WHAP WHAP WHAP WHAP
I DON'T *LIKE* FOOD COOKED OUT, DO YOU?
UGH. IT ALL TASTES THE SAME.
CRUNCH CRUNCH

FLOWERS ARE PRETTY STUPID.
SEE, IT'S A BRIGHT, SUNNY DAY OUT, RIGHT?
WELL, WITH THIS WATERING CAN, I CAN MAKE THEM THINK IT'S RAINING.
IT'S FUN TO MESS WITH THEIR MINDS.
WATTERSON

THE EXPERIMENT HAS GONE HORRIBLY WRONG! CALVIN HAS MUTATED INTO A GIANT FLY!
HE ZIPS ABOUT IN PARASITIC HUNGER, SEARCHING FOR DECAYING FLESH!
AN UNBEARABLE STENCH FILLS THE AIR. THE HIDEOUS BUG ZEROES IN.
WATTERSON
MMM! THIS MAKES ME HUNGRY!
DON'T BE GROSS. JUST TAKE OUT THE GARBAGE LIKE I ASKED YOU, WILL YOU PLEASE?

Calvin and Hobbes
by WATTERSON
IT'S ANOTHER NEW MORNING FOR MR. MONROE. HE GLANCES AT THE NEWSPAPER HEADLINES OVER A CUP OF COFFEE, AND GETS IN HIS RED SPORTS CAR TO GO TO WORK.
LITTLE DOES HE REALIZE IT'S HIS LAST DAY ON THE FACE OF THE EARTH!
CALVIN DRINKS THE MAGIC ELIXIR AND BEGINS AN INCREDIBLE TRANSFORMATION!
INSTANTLY HE GROWS! BIGGER AND BIGGER! HIGHER AND HIGHER!
HE IS NOW OVER 300 FEET TALL! THE FORMULA IS A SUCCESS!
CALVIN, THE MIGHTY GIANT, GOES ON A TERRIBLE RAMPAGE, STRIKING FEAR INTO THE HEARTS OF THE POPULACE!
NOTHING CAN STOP HIM! IT'S PANIC IN THE STREETS! A TOWN LIES IN RUINS!
NO, I WON'T BUY YOU ANY MORE TOY CARS. I SAW YOU! YOU DELIBERATELY STOMPED ON THOSE!
WATTERSON

C'MON, CALVIN! I SIGNED YOU UP FOR SWIMMING LESSONS.
I DON'T WANT SWIMMING LESSONS!!
TOO LATE. LET'S GO.
WHAT ABOUT HOBBES? DID YOU SIGN HIM UP TOO?
NO, IT'S NOT GOOD TO GET TIGERS WET.
WHY IS THAT?
IT TAKES US ALL DAY TO DRY, AND UNTIL WE DO, WE SMELL FUNNY.

I CAN'T BELIEVE MY MOM SIGNED ME UP FOR SWIMMING LESSONS.
HERE I AM FREEZING MY BUNS OFF AT 9 IN THE MORNING, ABOUT TO JUMP INTO ICE WATER AND DROWN.
THE ONLY THING THAT COULD POSSIBLY MAKE THIS WORSE WOULD BE IF THE CLASS WAS...
...TAUGHT BY MY SADISTIC BABY SITTER!!
WELL, LOOK WHO'S HERE!

OK... EVERYONE IN THE WATER!
I REFUSE! I'M FREEZING ALREADY!
CALVIN, DO YOU KNOW WHAT A "RAT TAIL" IS?
NO.
IT'S WHEN YOU SOAK A TOWEL AND TWIST IT UP INTO A WHIP. IT STINGS LIKE CRAZY AND IS MUCH WORSE THAN BEING COLD. GET MY DRIFT?
I ALWAYS THOUGHT LIFE-GUARDS WERE JUST TAUGHT HOW TO RESUSCITATE PEOPLE AND THINGS LIKE THAT.

THIS WATER IS FREEZING! I'M GOING TO GO INTO SHOCK AND DROWN, I JUST KNOW IT.
I BET THE LIFEGUARD IS INVOLVED IN SOME INSURANCE SCAM AND SHE'S GOING TO LET US ALL DROWN LIKE RATS! OH NO! OH NO!
WATTERSON
OK, FIRST WE'RE GOING TO LEARN THE "DEADMAN'S FLOAT."
MOM!! HELPP! HELPP!
WHAT I PUT UP WITH TO PAY FOR COLLEGE..

I DON'T WANT TO LEARN HOW TO SWIM!
I DON'T NEED TO KNOW HOW. I'LL JUST STAY ON DRY LAND ALL MY LIFE.
WHAT IF YOU FALL OUT OF A BOAT?
NO BIG DEAL.
WATTERSON

FORTY MINUTES OF TERROR! WHY DID YOU SIGN ME UP FOR THIS?
WHY NOT SOMETHING FUN, LIKE HANG GLIDING OR SHARPSHOOTING?
...OR DRIVING LESSONS! I COULD BE TAKING DRIVING LESSONS AND LEARNING SOMETHING USEFUL!
HOW ABOUT PIANO LESSONS? YOU START TUESDAY.
ACK!
NO NO NO NO NO NO NO NO NO NO NO
WATTERSON

Calvin and Hobbes
by WATTERSON
HEY, MOM, ARE YOU NERVOUS?
NO. ... WHY?
CALVIN, GO OUTSIDE AND QUIT BUGGING ME!
CALVIN THE BUG BUZZES OFF!
FLYING LOW OVER THE GRASS, HE SEARCHES FOR DEAD MEAT!
WATTERSON
UP AND OVER THE FLOWERS, DARTING THIS WAY AND THAT!
OH NO! HE'S CAUGHT IN A SPIDER WEB!
THRASHING ABOUT IN A DESPERATE BID FOR FREEDOM, HE ONLY BECOMES MORE ENTANGLED! SOON THE SPIDER WILL SUCK OUT HIS INNARDS! HELP!
I WAS GOING TO JOIN YOU IN THE HAMMOCK, BUT I THINK I'LL FORGET IT.

HI, CALVIN, WHAT ARE YOU DOING?
BIG IMPORTANT SECRET THINGS! GO AWAY! GET LOST!
ALL RIGHT, DANDELION HEAD! WHO CARES WHAT YOU DO ANYWAY!
WE'RE DOING GREAT THINGS. *WE'RE* HAVING **FUN**!
I THOUGHT WE WERE BORED OUT OF OUR SKULLS.
OH HUSH. YOU DON'T KNOW ANYTHING.
WATTERSON

THAT STUPID CALVIN. HE'S SO MEAN.
ALL I TRY TO DO IS BE FRIENDS, AND HE TREATS ME LIKE I'M NOBODY.
WELL, WHO NEEDS JERKS LIKE HIM ANYWAY? I DON'T NEED HIM FOR A FRIEND. I CAN HAVE FUN BY MYSELF!
POOP.
WATTERSON

SUSIE, HOBBES THOUGHT I WAS RUDE, SO I'M SORRY, AND YOU CAN COME PLAY WITH US IF YOU WANT.
THANKS, CALVIN. THAT'S REALLY NICE OF YOU.
OK, WE'LL PLAY HOUSE NOW. I'LL BE THE HIGH-POWERED EXECUTIVE WIFE, THE TIGER HERE CAN BE MY UNEMPLOYED, HOUSEKEEPING HUSBAND, AND YOU CAN BE OUR BRATTY AND BRAINLESS KID IN A DAY CARE CENTER.
THIS WAS *YOUR* IDEA, PEA BRAIN.
DON'T YOU TALK TO YOUR FATHER THAT WAY!
I'M OFF TO WALL STREET. DON'T WAIT UP.
WATTERSON

THE ALIENS ARE GAINING ON OUR HERO! IN A SURPRISE MOVE, SPACEMAN SPIFF SHIFTS INTO REVERSE!
THE ALIENS ROAR AHEAD! SPIFF SHIFTS BACK INTO FORWARD, AND PURSUES THE ALIENS!
...BUT THE ALIENS HAVE TURNED AROUND AND ARE HEADED STRAIGHT FOR OUR HERO! SPIFF SHIFTS INTO REVERSE!
I'M GETTING SICK.
WATTERSON

WHACK!
? ? ? ?
TELL ME THIS ISN'T A SPITBALL!!
WATTERSON

HOBBES, QUICK! HOW DO I STOP?!?
STEER INTO A GRAVEL DRIVEWAY AND FALL DOWN!
SKRUNCH!
THAT WAS ONLY A SUGGESTION.
WATTERSON

Calvin and HOBBES
by WATTERSON
BOY, IT'S QUIET AROUND HERE TODAY!
TOO QUIET!
HA HA! GOTCHA!
HEY!
SQUIRT!
SQUIRT!
..RRRRRRRR...
SQUEAK
WHOOSH!
HA HA! GOTCHA BACK!
HEY!
SPLOOSH
A WATER BALLOON! THAT DIRTY TIGER ESCALATED THE WAR! THIS CALLS FOR SUPREME RETALIATION!
I'LL GET HIM WITH THE GARDEN HOSE! NOTHING CAN BEAT A HOSE FOR SHEER VOLUME OF WATER!
...UNLESS, OF COURSE, HE WENT SO FAR AS TO...
WATTERSON

LOOK AT THAT THING IN THE DIRT! IT MUST BE A FOSSIL!
I WONDER WHAT PECULIAR ANIMAL ***THIS*** WAS.
BUT IT'S NOT A BONE. IT MUST BE SOME PRIMITIVE HUNTING WEAPON OR EATING UTENSIL FOR CAVE MEN.
WATTERSON
MAYBE IT HAD SOME RELIGIOUS FUNCTION.
THIS EXPLAINS WHY YOUR CLOTHES STAY ON THE FLOOR.

MAKING A SIGN?
I'M DECLARING THE CREEK BACK IN THE WOODS "CALVIN'S CREEK."
WHEN YOU DISCOVER SOMETHING, YOU'RE ALLOWED TO NAME IT AND PUT UP A SIGN.
Calvins CrEEK
BUT SUPPOSE YOU DIDN'T DISCOVER THAT CREEK.
OF COURSE I DID! NOBODY ***ELSE*** HAS A SIGN THERE, RIGHT?
Hobs Crk
WATTERSON

CAN HOBBES AND I GO PLAY IN THE RAIN, MOM?
NO.
WHY NOT?
YOU'LL GET SOAKED.
WHAT'S WRONG WITH THAT?
YOU COULD CATCH PNEUMONIA, RUN UP A TERRIBLE HOSPITAL BILL, LINGER A FEW MONTHS, AND DIE.
I ALWAYS FORGET. IF YOU ASK A MOM, YOU GET A WORST-CASE SCENARIO.
I HAD NO IDEA THESE LITTLE SHOWERS WERE SO ***DANGEROUS.***
WATTERSON

WANT TO GO SPELUNKING WITH ME?
SPELUNKING? THERE AREN'T ANY CAVES AROUND HERE!
YOU DON'T NEED A CAVE. ALL YOU NEED IS A ROCK.
SPELUNK!

WELL DAD, OFF TO WORK?
TOO BAD. *I'M* ON SUMMER VACATION, SO *I* GET TO STAY HOME AND DO WHATEVER I WANT.
WELL, GO OFF AND JOIN THE RAT RACE! MOM AND I ARE RACKING UP LOTS OF EXPENSES!
OOG.
I JUST DO THAT TO HELP HIM APPRECIATE THE WEEKENDS MORE.

HOT DAY, ISN'T IT?
I'LL SAY.
BUT IT'S THE HUMIDITY THAT REALLY GETS TO ME.
YOU DON'T LIKE IT WHEN IT'S HUMID?
NOT AT ALL.
THEN YOU'D BETTER GET OUT QUICK.

Calvin and Hobbes
by WATTERSON
GO ON "THREE," OK? ONE..... TWO.....
TWO AND A HALF...
OOMF!
READY.... SET....
GO!
PIT PAT PIT PAT PIT
PAT PIT PAT PIT PAT
PITTIDA DITTIDA PITTIDA DITTIDA
CHOOGA CHOOGA CHOOGA
EEEE
NYEEOWWW
GASP I CAN'T BELIEVE IT! NO SONIC BOOM! NOT EVEN A "POP"!
I HEARD A POP, BUT I THINK IT WAS MY LUNGS.
WATTERSON

WHAT'S FOR DINNER?
SALMON.
SALMON?! BLECCHH!!
CALVIN, ONE OF THESE DAYS YOUR FACE IS GOING TO FREEZE LIKE THAT.
WOW!
WATTERSON

HI, HOBBES!
GOOD HEAVENS, WHAT'S WRONG WITH *YOU*?
MOM SAID IF I KEEP MAKING THIS FACE, IT WILL FREEZE LIKE THIS FOREVER!
YOU REALLY THINK SO?
IT'S WORTH A TRY...
WATTERSON
I'LL BET MY FEATURES ARE HARDENING ALREADY.
I ALWAYS LIKED GARGOYLES.

DON'T MAKE FACES AT THE TABLE, CALVIN.
I CAN'T HELP IT.
MOM SAID MY FACE WOULD FREEZE LIKE THIS SOME DAY, AND IT JUST DID.
NO, IT DIDN'T.
IT DID, DAD! MOM WAS RIGHT. I'M HORRIBLY DISFIGURED FOR LIFE.
NO, YOU AREN'T.
BUT DON'T WORRY, I WON'T SPOIL DINNER. SEE? ELEPHANT MAN!
WATTERSON

HERE COMES SUSIE.
HA! WON'T SHE BE HORRIFIED TO SEE HOW OUR FACES HAVE TRAGICALLY FROZEN!
HI, SUSIE.
HI, CALVIN.
WHAT DID YOU DO, GET YOUR HEAD STUCK IN THE BLENDER? IT'S AN IMPROVEMENT.
WATTERSON

ARE THE COALS HOT?
YES, THEY'RE VERY HOT. I'M JUST ABOUT TO PUT ON THE HAMBURGERS.
BEFORE YOU DO, COULD YOU TOSS IN THE CAN OF LIGHTER FLUID AND MAKE A GIANT FIREBALL?
I'VE GOT THE MOST BORING DAD IN THE WORLD.
WATTERSON

WITH THESE SNORKELS, WE CAN STAY UNDER WATER INDEFINITELY.
JUST THINK OF ALL THE FISH WE'LL BE ABLE TO SEE!
WE CAN COLLECT SHELLS!
LET'S GO!
WELL SO FAR, THIS HAS BEEN A MAJOR DISAPPOINTMENT.
WATTERSON

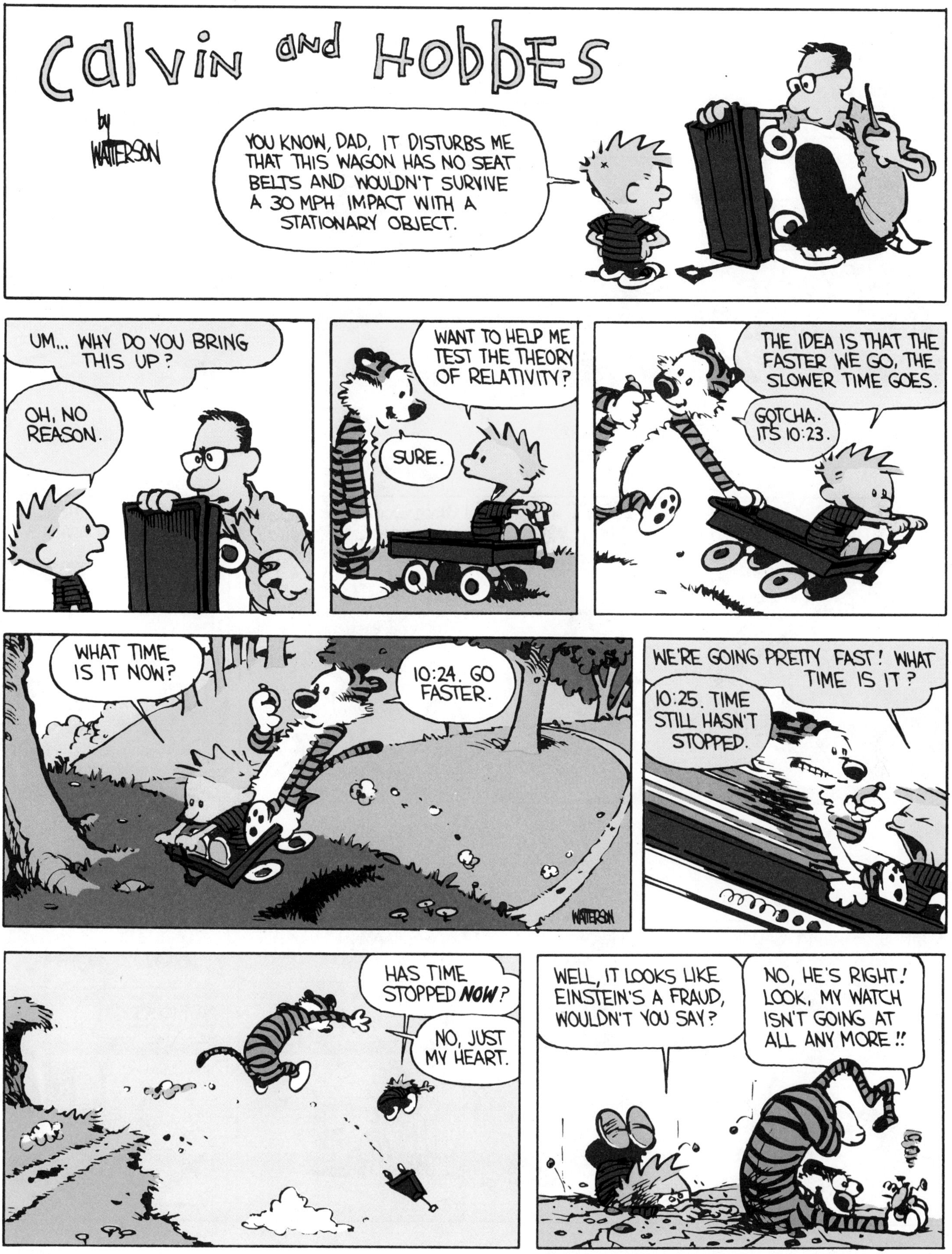
Calvin and HOBBES
by WATTERSON
YOU KNOW, DAD, IT DISTURBS ME THAT THIS WAGON HAS NO SEAT BELTS AND WOULDN'T SURVIVE A 30 MPH IMPACT WITH A STATIONARY OBJECT.
UM... WHY DO YOU BRING THIS UP?
OH, NO REASON.
WANT TO HELP ME TEST THE THEORY OF RELATIVITY?
SURE.
THE IDEA IS THAT THE FASTER WE GO, THE SLOWER TIME GOES.
GOTCHA. ITS 10:23.
WHAT TIME IS IT NOW?
10:24. GO FASTER.
WATTERSON
WE'RE GOING PRETTY FAST! WHAT TIME IS IT?
10:25. TIME STILL HASN'T STOPPED.
HAS TIME STOPPED *NOW*?
NO, JUST MY HEART.
WELL, IT LOOKS LIKE EINSTEIN'S A FRAUD, WOULDN'T YOU SAY?
NO, HE'S RIGHT! LOOK, MY WATCH ISN'T GOING AT ALL ANY MORE!!

"ADD TWO EGGS AND STIR."
RIGHT.
THE RECIPE SAYS IT MAKES TWENTY PANCAKES, SO WE'LL EACH GET TEN.
NAH, THAT'S TOO MUCH TROUBLE.
WE'LL JUST MAKE ONE BIG PANCAKE AND CUT IT IN HALF.
WATTERSON

DAD, I WANT A BEDTIME STORY!
I'M BUSY, CALVIN. I'LL READ YOU ONE TOMORROW.
IF YOU DON'T READ ME A STORY, I WON'T GO TO BED!
Once upon a time there was a boy named Calvin, who always wanted things his way. One day his dad got sick of it and locked him in the basement for the rest of his life. Everyone else lived happily ever after.
The End.
I DON'T LIKE THESE STORIES WITH MORALS.
WATTERSON

DINNER'S READY, CALVIN. COME TO THE TABLE.
I'M WATCHING TELEVISION.
NO, YOU'RE NOT!
YES, I AM. I'M RIGHT HERE IN FRONT OF IT!
NO YOU'RE NOT!
OH THAT'S RIGHT. I'M AT THE TABLE.
WATTERSON

I SAW A TURTLE DOWN BY THE CREEK.
BIG DEAL! WHO CARES? I'VE SEEN HUNDREDS OF TURTLES! PROBABLY MILLIONS! WHO WANTS TO SEE ANOTHER DUMB OL' TURTLE?
HA!
WATTERSON

CAN I RIDE IN THE GROCERY CART?
I THINK YOU'RE A LITTLE BIG FOR THAT NOW.
PLEASE?!?
ALL RIGHT. UP YOU GO.
OH BOY!
NOW RUN DOWN THE AISLE AND LET GO!
WATTERSON

AAWWEEEAWWEEAAW!
THE WATER LOOKED A LITTLE COLD, EH, TARZAN?
WATTERSON

Calvin and HobbEs
by WATTERSON
WANNA TOSS THE OL' PIGSKIN AROUND?
HECK NO.
PHOOEY.
THE CENTER SNAPS THE BALL!
THE QUARTERBACK LOOKS FOR AN OPENING!
THE DEFENSE DISINTEGRATES BENEATH THE COMING ONSLAUGHT! THE QUARTER-BACK JUMPS AND DODGES!
HOBBES BREAKS CLEAR!
CALVIN PASSES!
AN AMAZING CATCH! HOBBES IS AT THE 30...THE 20...THE 10..
...BUT HE'S TACKLED FROM BEHIND AND LATERALS TO CALVIN SO HE CAN MAKE THE TOUCHDOWN!
BUT CALVIN FUMBLES THE BALL AND HOBBES RECOVERS IT!
BUT A PENALTY IS CALLED ON THE PLAY AND HOBBES IS SENT TO THE BENCH!
HOBBES DEFECTS TO THE OTHER TEAM AND IS GREETED WITH ENTHUSIASTIC CHEERS! THE CROWD GOES WILD!
!
CALVIN PREPARES TO CRIPPLE THE TRAITOR WITH AN ILLEGAL FACE MASK PULL!
HOBBES DEFIES HIM BY POURING OUT HIS MOUTH GUARD ONTO CALVIN'S HELMET!
BOY, YOU CAN SEE WHY FOOTBALL IS SUCH A VIOLENT GAME!
HOBBES' TEAM GAINS A YARD! ALL THE CHEER-LEADERS COME OUT FOR SMOOCHES!!
WATTERSON

I THINK I'M USING TOO STRONG A SUN SCREEN.
WATTERSON

FISHING IS THE MOST BORING SPORT IN THE WORLD.
WE'VE BEEN SITTING HERE FOR TWENTY MINUTES AND NOT ONE THING HAS HAPPENED!
WAAUGHH
WATTERSON

YOU'RE ON MY HALF OF THE BED! MOVE OVER!
YOUR SIDE IS WAY OVER THERE! GIVE ME BACK THOSE COVERS!
CALVIN, BE QUIET AND GO TO SLEEP!!
WATTERSON
YOU HEARD DAD. HE SAID TO GET ON YOUR SIDE AND LEAVE THE COVERS ALONE!
THAT'S NOT WHAT HE SAID! HEY! YOU STOLE MY PILLOW! THIS LUMPY ONE IS YOURS!

WITH A DRINK OF MAGIC ELIXIR, CALVIN TURNS HIMSELF INVISIBLE.
COMPLETELY TRANSPARENT, HE ROAMS UNDETECTED!
CALVIN?
BOY, AS SOON AS YOU WANT SOMETHING DONE AROUND HERE, THAT KID'S NOWHERE TO BE SEEN.

HA HA! I HAVE TURNED MYSELF INVISIBLE!
BY REMOVING MY CLOTHING, I CAN PERPETRATE ANY CRIME UNDETECTED!
I HAVE COMPLETE FREEDOM! I CAN GET AWAY WITH ANYTHING!
CALVIN! WHAT ON EARTH ARE YOU DOING IN THE COOKIE JAR WITHOUT YOUR CLOTHES ON?!?

YOUR POLLS ARE SLIPPING, DAD. BETTER GET WITH IT.
CALVIN, BEING YOUR DAD IS NOT AN ELECTED POSITION. I DON'T HAVE TO RESPOND TO POLLS.
NOT ELECTED? YOU MEAN YOU CAN GOVERN WITH DICTATORIAL IMPUNITY?
EXACTLY.
IN SHORT, OPEN REVOLT AND EXILE IS THE ONLY HOPE FOR CHANGE?
I DON'T LIKE THE DIRECTION THIS CONVERSATION IS TAKING..

Calvin and Hobbes
by WATTERSON
GRAVITY IS ARBITRARY!
CALVIN WAKES UP ONE DAY TO FIND HE IS IMMUNE TO THE FORCE OF GRAVITY.
HE HANGS ON TO THE GROUND FOR DEAR LIFE, BUT HIS GRIP IS WEAKENING!
HE CAN'T HOLD ON! HE... HE LETS GO!
AAAAAAAAAAA
HIGHER AND HIGHER, AS UPWARD HE FALLS!
ONLY BY GRABBING THE TAIL FIN OF A PASSING JET DOES CALVIN SAVE HIMSELF FROM BEING HURLED OUT INTO SPACE!
WATTERSON
NO, NO, LET HIM FINISH. THIS IS VERY INTERESTING. SO AFTER YOU LANDED IN PHOENIX, WHAT HAPPENED?
WELL, I DON'T CARE. I'M NOT SEWING VELCRO ON THE OUTSIDE OF ALL HIS CLOTHES.
WELL, ABOUT THEN MY GRAVITY CAME BACK, SO I...

I'M GOING TO LEARN HOW TO RIDE THIS BICYCLE EVEN IF IT KILLS ME.
OK, YOU CAN LET GO...
AAUGH!
DID IT KILL YOU?
NOT YET. IT'S DECIDED TO MAIM ME FIRST.

THEY SAY ONCE YOU LEARN HOW TO RIDE A BICYCLE, YOU NEVER FORGET.
THAT DOESN'T SURPRISE ME.
WAARRGH!
IT WORKS ON THE SAME PRINCIPLE AS ELECTROSHOCK THERAPY.

EASY...EASY... HOLD IT STILL..
THERE! LOOK!
I DID IT! I'M BALANCING!
THAT'S GOOD. DO YOU WANT TO TRY IT WITH THE KICKSTAND UP?

CRASH!
IT JUMPED ME!!
WATTERSON

LOOK, THERE'S A FROG!
C'MON, LET'S CATCH IT!
I'M NOT GETTING NEAR IT.
WHY NOT?
THEY DRINK WATER ALL DAY JUST IN CASE SOMEONE PICKS THEM UP.
WATTERSON

I'M GOING TO HANG AROUND THE DRUGSTORE ALL AFTERNOON AND EAT CANDY AND READ COMIC BOOKS!
OH, NO, YOU'RE NOT!
WHY NOT?!
BECAUSE I'M YOUR MOTHER AND I SAID SO. GET BACK IN HERE.
AND YOU CAN STOP GOOSE-STEPPING AROUND THE HOUSE!
WATTERSON

Calvin and Hobbes
by WATTERSON
DO YOU THINK BOOGEYMEN REALLY EXIST?
I DON'T KNOW.
..BUT IF THEY DO, I'M SURE THIS IS WHERE THEY LIVE.
THAT WAS THE CREEPIEST CAMPFIRE STORY I'VE EVER HEARD. LET'S GET BACK TO THE TENT!
I DON'T THINK I'LL EVER SLEEP AGAIN.
SHH!
WHAT? DID YOU HEAR SOMETHING ??
DIDN'T YOU?
I DON'T KNOW. WHAT DID IT SOUND LIKE?
SORT OF LIKE BREATHING AND DROOLING AND RIPPING THE MEAT OFF HUMAN BONES!
YAAHHHH
YOU WERE RIGHT. I'M GLAD WE CARRIED A GENERATOR ALL THIS DISTANCE.
WATTERSON

HEY, MOM, CAN WE GO OUT FOR PIZZA TONIGHT?
NO, WE HAD PIZZA LAST NIGHT, AND BESIDES, IT'S TOO EXPENSIVE TO EAT OUT ALL THE TIME.
OH, YOU'D RATHER BLOW THE EVENING COOKING AND WASHING DISHES THAN SPEND A FEW BUCKS?
WATTERSON
IT SEEMS LIKE WE GO OUT FOR PIZZA A LOT THESE DAYS.
IF YOU'D RATHER FIX A DISH OF CEREAL AT HOME, BE MY GUEST.
HOBBES WANTS TRIPLE ANCHOVIES.

CALVIN AND HIS TRUSTY NAVIGATOR HOBBES ROAR DOWN THE RESIDENTIAL ROAD AT 90 MPH!
HOBBES PUTS ON THE TURN SIGNAL.
FASTER AND FASTER THEY GO! A BUSLOAD OF SCHOOLCHILDREN DIVES FROM THE SIDEWALK!
HOBBES PUTS ON THE WINDSHIELD WIPERS.
THE POLICE ARE AFTER THEM! CALVIN CRAWLS DOWN TO PUT IN THE CLUTCH AND SHIFT!
HOBBES STEERS AND BLOWS THE HORN!
ALL RIGHT, I'M BACK ALREADY! CAN'T I EVEN RUN AN ERRAND WITHOUT YOU BLOWING THE HORN ACROSS THE PARKING LOT?!
IT WAS HOBBES, MOM. NOT ME.
WATTERSON

SEE ANY UFOs?
NOT YET.
WELL, KEEP YOUR EYES PEELED. THEY'RE BOUND TO LAND HERE SOONER OR LATER.
WHAT WILL WE DO WHEN THEY COME?
SEE IF WE CAN SELL MOM AND DAD INTO SLAVERY FOR A STAR CRUISER.
WATTERSON

Z
YAWN!
!
TA DAA!
SHEESH.
WATTERSON

CALVIN, I DON'T WANT YOU UP IN THAT TREE.
WHY NOT?
SOME OF THE BRANCHES ARE DEAD AND THEY MIGHT BREAK. COME ON DOWN.
MOM SPOILS EVERYTHING.
THIS ISN'T QUITE THE SAME, IS IT?
WATTERSON

GLOONK!
GLOONK!
CALVIN, DRINK YOUR MILK IN LITTLE SIPS!
WATTERSON

Calvin and HOBBES
by WATTERSON
SPACEMAN SPIFF IS HIT! HE'S GOING DOWN!
FORTUNATELY, OUR HERO ALWAYS BUCKLES UP!
THE FEARLESS SPACEMAN SPIFF HAS CRASHED ON A DISTANT WORLD!
WATTERSON
THE PLANET'S ATMOSPHERE IS THICK WITH NOXIOUS FUMES AND GASES! OUR HERO CAN HARDLY BREATHE.
SPIFF MUST FIND HELP QUICKLY... BUT IS THERE ANY LIFE ON THIS HOSTILE WORLD?
HIS QUESTION IS ANSWERED WHEN A HIDEOUS BLOB OF GELATINOUS MUCK OOZES OUT OF A CREVICE TOWARD HIM!
SPIFF'S BLASTER IS USELESS AGAINST THE SLIME!
OUR HERO TRIES TO ESCAPE, BUT THE SUFFOCATING STENCH ENVELOPS HIM! WHAT A DISGUSTING FATE!
YECHHH I SURE WISH I'D BROUGHT MY LUNCH TODAY!
THAT'S GROSS, CALVIN! IF YOU DON'T LIKE THE CAFETERIA'S TAPIOCA, JUST LEAVE IT ALONE!

SUMMER VACATION'S OVER! NOTHING AHEAD BUT TOIL AND DRUDGERY FOR A WHOLE YEAR!
OH, COME ON, YOU SPENT HALF THE SUMMER COMPLAINING HOW BORED YOU WERE.
I DID?
YOU DID.
HOW STRANGE. I MUST HAVE BEEN DELIRIOUS FROM HAVING SO MUCH FUN.
WATTERSON

I CAN'T BELIEVE IT! HOMEWORK ALREADY! I JUST GOT BACK TO SCHOOL!
I HAVE TO WRITE A PARAGRAPH ON WHAT I DID OVER THE SUMMER! A WHOLE PARAGRAPH!!
I'LL NEVER BE ABLE TO WRITE THAT MUCH! IT'S NOT FAIR!!
WATTERSON
HOW'S IT COMING?
NOT SO GOOD. WHAT DID YOU DO BESIDES WATCH TV?

IN SOCCER, YOU CAN'T TOUCH THE BALL WITH YOUR HANDS OR ARMS.
SEE, YOU CAN USE ANY OTHER PART OF YOUR BODY...
...EVEN YOUR HEAD!
WATTERSON
YEAH, BUT YOUR FACE?? DOESN'T THAT HURT?
RRRRGHH! THAT'S NOT WHAT I MEANT TO DO!

I HAVE A HYPOTHETICAL QUESTION. SUPPOSE A KID AT SCHOOL CALLED ME A NASTY NAME...
...SHOULD I KICK HIM REAL HARD IN THE SHINS?
NO, I DON'T THINK VIOLENCE WOULD BE JUSTIFIED.
HERE'S ANOTHER HYPOTHETICAL QUESTION. WHAT IF I ALREADY DID?
WATTERSON

I'VE DECIDED TO GROW A BEARD, MOM.
A LONG BEARD. LIKE THE GUYS IN ZZ TOP.
THAT'S NICE, CALVIN. YOU GO AHEAD AND DO THAT.
I THOUGHT SHE'D PUT UP MORE OF A FUSS THAN THAT.
WATTERSON

HOW ABOUT THESE PANTS, MOM? CAN I GET THESE?
GOOD HEAVENS, LOOK AT THE PRICE! I DON'T HAVE PANTS THAT COST THIS MUCH!
AND YOU'LL GROW RIGHT OUT OF THESE! HONESTLY, WHY WOULD ANY KID NEED DESIGNER CLOTHES??
BABES, MOM. I GOTTA LOOK COOL.
"BABES."
WATTERSON

Calvin and HOBBES
by WATTERSON
DON'T TURN OUT THE LIGHT, DAD! YOU DIDN'T CHECK UNDER THE BED FOR MONSTERS!
I'M SURE THERE ARE NO MONSTERS UNDER YOUR BED. GO TO SLEEP.
GOOD NIGHT.
GOOD-BYE.
ANY MONSTERS UNDER MY BED TONIGHT?
THERE'S NO ANSWER. DO YOU THINK THEY'RE GONE?
MAYBE THEY'RE JUST STAYING QUIET. KEEP WATCH OVER THE SIDE OF THE BED..
BOY, AM I FULL! I MUST'VE GAINED TEN POUNDS TODAY! MAYBE I'M GETTING A LITTLE PLUMP!
WATTERSON
YOU'RE BIGGER, CALVIN, BUT THERE'S NO FAT ON YOU!
I GUESS YOU'RE RIGHT. I'M GETTING BIG, BUT I'M STILL NICE AND LEAN!
UGH. SOMETHING UNDER THE BED IS DROOLING.
START TYING THE SHEETS TOGETHER. WE'LL GO OUT THE WINDOW.

Pay up, Squirt.
FORGET IT, MOE. I'M NOT GIVING YOU MONEY.
IN FACT, I DON'T EVEN HAVE ANY.
Gee, that's too bad.
OH WAIT, YES, I DO! HERE.
FOR A KID WITH A MONOSYLLABIC VOCABULARY, HE'S AWFULLY PERSUASIVE.
WATTERSON

OK, HOBBES, HERE'S THE PLAN TO PUT MOE OUT OF COMMISSION.
YOU COME TO SCHOOL WITH ME, AND WHEN MOE COMES TO STEAL MY MONEY, YOU JUMP OUT AND EAT HIM!
WATTERSON
EAT HIM?? I COULDN'T DO THAT!
SURE YOU COULD! WHAT'S WRONG WITH THAT?!
FAT KIDS ARE HIGH IN CHOLESTEROL.
WELL, JUST CHEW HIM UP AND SPIT HIM OUT, I DON'T CARE!!

IF THAT BULLY IS EXTORTING MONEY, I'M GOING TO CALL THE SCHOOL AND PUT AN END TO IT.
DON'T DO THAT! IF MOE FINDS OUT I SQUEALED, I'M A GONER!
WATTERSON
THIS KID CAN'T GET AWAY WITH STEALING, CALVIN. SOMEBODY'S GOT TO DO SOMETHING.
HERE'S A LIST OF WHAT I'M WEARING. SEE YOU AT THE MORGUE.

Hey, Twinkie, here's the 25¢ I "borrowed" from you the other day.
Somebody ratted on me, and it's gonna be a dark day if I ever find out who!
I THINK I'LL USE THE QUARTER TO CALL MY INSURANCE AGENT.
WATTERSON

HI, DAD, IT'S ME!
CALVIN, IS THIS IMPORTANT? I'M VERY BUSY THIS MORNING.
I'LL MAKE IT FAST, DAD. CAN YOU PICK UP SOME TOPSOIL AND GRASS SEED ON YOUR WAY HOME?
OK, SURE. GOODBYE.
WATTERSON

RING
RING
WATTERSON
HELLO, CALVIN SPEAKING. I'D LIKE TO ORDER A LARGE ANCHOVY PIZZA.
WHAT? I...??
OH, I'M SORRY. YOU MUST HAVE DIALED THE WRONG NUMBER. GOODBYE.
I TRY TO MAKE EVERYONE'S DAY A LITTLE MORE SURREAL.

Calvin and Hobbes
by WATTERSON
QUIT SQUIRMING, CALVIN. YOU'VE GOT ICE CREAM ALL OVER YOUR SHIRT.
RATS, I WAS SAVING IT FOR LATER.
THANKS FOR THE ICE CREAM, DAD. IT WAS GREAT.
YOU'RE WELCOME.
I'M TIRED OF PULLING YOU. IT'S MY TURN TO RIDE.
YOUR DAD DIDN'T GET ME ANY ICE CREAM, SO I GET TO RIDE BOTH WAYS.
NO, YOU DON'T! DAD SAID TIGERS DON'T LIKE ICE CREAM! IT'S MY TURN TO RIDE!
TIGERS DON'T KNOW IF THEY LIKE ICE CREAM UNTIL THEY TRY EVERY KIND. I'M NOT PULLING.
I'VE GOT NEWS, FUZZ BRAIN. I'M NOT PULLING, EITHER!
WELL THEN, I GUESS WE'LL BOTH JUST SIT HERE UNTIL WE DIE.
WATTERSON
WHY DO THESE "WALKS" ALWAYS END UP AS "RIDES"?
OH, YOU NEED THE EXERCISE MORE ANYWAY.

WHAT ARE YOU DOING?
BEING "COOL."
WATTERSON
YOU LOOK MORE LIKE YOU'RE BEING BORED.
THE WORLD BORES YOU WHEN YOU'RE COOL.

LOOK, I BROUGHT A SOMBRERO!
NOW WE CAN *BOTH* BE "COOL"!
A SOMBRERO? ARE YOU CRAZY?! COOL PEOPLE DON'T WEAR SOMBREROS! ***NOBODY*** WEARS SOMBREROS!
WHAT FUN IS IT BEING "COOL" IF YOU CAN'T WEAR A SOMBRERO?
WATTERSON

I'M BACK. SEE, I PUT ON SOME MICKEY MOUSE PANTS!
I'LL BE "COOL" IN THESE, BOY. JUST LOOK AT THESE BIG YELLOW BUTTONS!
MICKEY MOUSE PANTS?!? YOU DON'T LOOK COOL! YOU LOOK LIKE AN IDIOT!
HMPH! MAYBE I'M NEW WAVE.
MAYBE YOU'RE JUST STUPID.
WATTERSON

HERE COMES SUSIE. I'M GOING TO THROW A PINE CONE AT HER.
WWHIPPPP
POW!
ZINGGG
WATTERSON

YAHH!
OOF! GRRR!
RGH!
RR!
RRR!
UH!
UH!
RRR!
UMPH!
TOUCHDOWN!
LET'S PLAY SOMETHING ELSE.
WATTERSON

ARE THERE ANY MONSTERS UNDER MY BED TONIGHT?
NO.
NOPE.
NO.
WATTERSON
IF THERE **WERE** ANY MONSTERS UNDER MY BED, HOW BIG WOULD THEY BE?
VERY SMALL. GO TO SLEEP.
MOMM!

Calvin and Hobbes
by WATTERSON
I'M HUNGRY. WHEN'S LUNCH?
RIGHT NOW.
HI, SUSIE!
OH LOOK, YOU'VE GOT YOUR STUFFED TIGER! CAN I SQUEEZE HIM?
WHAT ARE YOU, CRAZY? HOBBES IS A FEROCIOUS MAN-EATING JUNGLE BEAST!
FEROCIOUS? HE LOOKS FUZZY AND CUDDLY TO ME!
HA! BENEATH THAT SOFT EXTERIOR LIE TERRIBLE MANDIBLES OF BONE-CRUSHING DEATH! HE'LL GRIND YOU INTO HAMBURGER!
EACH MIGHTY PAW HIDES RAZOR-SHARP CLAWS TO RIP THE LIVING HIDE OFF ANY HUMAN THAT WANDERS TOO CLOSE! HE'S A MONSTER!
NO, HE'S NOT. HE'S A BIG CUTIE.
OH NO! I CAN'T LOOK!!
...SO WHAT HAPPENED TO THE MANDIBLES OF DEATH, YOU SISSY FURBALL?!?
I WAS BEGUILED BY HER FEMININE CHARMS. YOW.
GO SOAK YOUR HEAD.
WATTERSON

WITH GREAT EFFORT, CALVIN THE HUMAN INSECT ADVANCES THE PAPER IN THE TYPEWRITER.
HIS ONLY HOPE FOR PROPER MEDICAL TREATMENT LIES IN HIS ABILITY TO WRITE A LEGIBLE MESSAGE TO HIS FAMILY!
WATTERSON
HE CRAWLS TO EACH KEY AND JUMPS!
WHO WROTE "HELP I'M A BUG" ON MY LETTER TO GRANDMA?
EVIDENTLY SOME BUG. HOW STRANGE.

BACK AND FORTH.
BACK AND FORTH.
TIDAL WAVE!
WATTERSON
BEATS ME, MOM. MAYBE THE SEAL AROUND THE TUB LEAKS.

WHAT'S THIS MUSIC?
IT'S "THE 1812 OVERTURE."
I KINDA LIKE IT. INTERESTING PERCUSSION SECTION.
WATTERSON
THOSE ARE CANNONS.
AND THEY PERFORM THIS IN CROWDED CONCERT HALLS?? GEE, I THOUGHT CLASSICAL MUSIC WAS BORING!

BOY, WHAT A DAY!
I WENT TO SCHOOL, PLAYED OUTSIDE, AND DID MY HOMEWORK. I'M EXHAUSTED.
YOU KNOW WHAT TIME IT IS NOW?
UH, 7:35.
IT'S MILLER TIME.
GET BACK HERE.
WATTERSON

PSST... SUSIE! WHAT'S 12 + 7?
A BILLION.
THANKS!
WAIT A MINUTE. THAT CAN'T BE RIGHT...
THAT'S WHAT SHE SAID 3+4 WAS.
WATTERSON

I JUST READ THIS GREAT SCIENCE FICTION STORY.
IT'S ABOUT HOW MACHINES TAKE CONTROL OF HUMANS AND TURN THEM INTO ZOMBIE SLAVES!
SO INSTEAD OF US CONTROLLING MACHINES, THEY CONTROL US? PRETTY SCARY IDEA.
I'LL SAY. HEY! WHAT TIME IS IT?? MY TV SHOW IS ON!
WATTERSON

Calvin and Hobbes
by WATTERSON
WERE THERE DINOSAURS WHEN YOU WERE A KID, DAD?
OH SURE! YOUR GRANDFATHER AND I USED TO PUT ON OUR LEOPARD SKINS AND HUNT BRONTOSAURUS FOR ALL THE CLAN RITUALS.
LISTEN, BUSTER, I THINK CALVIN'S GRADES ARE BAD ENOUGH ALREADY, DON'T YOU?
THE HORRIFYING TYRANNOSAURUS LUMBERS ACROSS THE PREHISTORIC VALLEY.
THE MIGHTY DINOSAUR IS A WALKING DEATH MACHINE!
ONLY ONE OTHER CREATURE DARES TO CHALLENGE THE TERRIBLE TYRANNOSAURUS!
...THE SAVAGE SABER-TOOTHED TIGER!
UNK GZZ...
GG *MMF* YOW GZZZ
MKN GBZZ.. YOW...
WATTERSON
WAKE UP!
THE MEEK TYRANNOSAURUS, VICTIM OF AN INNOCENT MISUNDERSTANDING, TEARS LIKE HECK ACROSS THE PREHISTORIC VALLEY..

TOMORROW WE'RE GOING TO DISCUSS "CURRENT EVENTS" IN SCHOOL.
EACH OF US HAS TO FIND A NEWSPAPER ARTICLE, READ IT TO THE CLASS, AND EXPLAIN IT.
WATTERSON
WHAT ARTICLE DID YOU CHOOSE?
THIS ONE.
"SPACE ALIEN WEDS TWO-HEADED ELVIS CLONE."
ACTUALLY, THERE'S NOT MUCH LEFT TO EXPLAIN.

LOOK WHAT YOU CAN DO WITH BIG SOCKS!
JUST PUT ONE OVER EACH EAR, AND ONE OVER YOUR NOSE...
AN ELEPHANT! HA HA! I WANT SOME SOCKS TOO!
WATTERSON
IF I MISS THE BUS, IT'S GOING TO BE UNPLEASANT AROUND HERE!

CALVIN, HOW DID YOU BREAK THIS DISH?!
I WAS CARRYING TOO MUCH AND IT DROPPED.
YOUR PROBLEM IS YOU'VE GOT NO COMMON SENSE.
I'VE GOT PLENTY OF COMMON SENSE!
I JUST CHOOSE TO IGNORE IT.
WATTERSON

I DON'T UNDERSTAND THIS BUSINESS ABOUT DEATH.
IF WE'RE JUST GOING TO DIE, WHAT'S THE POINT OF LIVING?
WELL, THERE'S SEAFOOD...
I DON'T KNOW WHY I EVEN **TALK** TO YOU BEFORE DINNER.
WATTERSON

I'VE DECIDED I WANT TO BE A MILLIONAIRE WHEN I GROW UP.
WELL, YOU'LL HAVE TO WORK PRETTY HARD TO GET A MILLION DOLLARS.
WATTERSON
NO, I WON'T. YOU WILL.
ME?
I JUST WANT TO INHERIT IT.

THE WORST PART ABOUT GOING TO SCHOOL IS WAITING FOR THE BUS.
ALL YOU CAN DO IS STAND HERE AND IMAGINE WHAT'S GOING TO GO WRONG DURING THE DAY. I BET WE HAVE A POP MATH QUIZ OR SOMETHING.
WELL, HERE COMES THE BUS. THANKS FOR WAITING WITH ME.
MY PLEASURE.
BOY, MY LUNCH BOX SEEMS LIGHT.
WATTERSON

Calvin and HOBBES
by WATTERSON
NOW WHERE DID ALL THE BED PILLOWS GO?
THIS IS GONNA BE SOFT!
KRUNCH
HEY, HOBBES! C'MON AND JUMP IN THE LEAVES! IT'S FUN!
I DON'T KNOW. SOMETIMES SLUGS HIDE UNDER LEAVES.
NO THEY DON'T. DO THEY? SLUGS?
UGH, JUST IMAGINE ONE OF THOSE SLIMY MUCKBALLS SLIPPING UP YOUR PANT LEG! THERE MIGHT BE DOZENS IN THERE!
THERE MIGHT?
AACK
YECCH
ICK
OOH
THAT'S THE PROBLEM WITH NATURE. SOMETHING'S ALWAYS STINGING YOU OR OOZING MUCOUS ON YOU. LET'S GO WATCH TV.
IS IT 3 O'CLOCK YET? WE CAN WATCH "THE BLOB"!
WATTERSON

AS YOU CAN SEE, SPACEMAN SPIFF, WE HAVE WAYS OF EXTRACTING INFORMATION FROM EVEN THE MOST UNCOOPERATIVE PRISONERS!
OUR HERO, CAPTURED BY ZORKONS, EYES THE DIABOLICAL INSTRUMENTS OF TORTURE!
VERY AMUSING, YOU TWISTED SPACE FROG. WHAT'S **THIS** FIENDISH DEVICE CALLED?
A CHIN-UP BAR. GET ON IT.
SPIFF READIES HIS DARING ESCAPE...
GYM INSTRUCTOR
WATTERSON

WHERE'S MY JACKET?
IT'S RIGHT ON THE FLOOR WHERE YOU LEFT IT.
IT'S STILL ON THE FLOOR? WHY DIDN'T YOU PUT IT AWAY?
WATTERSON
GEE, MY OWN COPY OF THE EMANCIPATION PROCLAMATION.

LOOK, I CAN MAKE SHADOWS ON THE WALL. HERE'S A DOG.
HEY, THAT'S GOOD!
HERE'S A SWAN.
HMM... THAT LOOKS MORE LIKE SOME BUG-EYED TENTACLED THING...
MOMMM!
WATTERSON

AH... AH... AH..
..AH...
KBTHCHH!
WHY'D YOU HOLD IT IN?
I'M TRYING TO BLOW MY SHOES OFF.

IT SAYS ON THE BACK OF THIS RECORD THAT THE COMPOSER COULD PLAY THE PIANO AT AGE THREE.
HE WROTE HIS FIRST SYMPHONY WHEN HE WAS FOUR.
THAT'S AMAZING.
WHEN I WAS FOUR, I THINK I WAS TOILET TRAINED.

I'M DONE WITH MY HOMEWORK!
I'M GOING OUTSIDE TO PLAY! I'VE GOT MY JACKET!
I'M LEAVING NOW!
...FURTHER BULLETINS AS EVENTS WARRANT!

Calvin and HOBBES
by WATTERSON
...SO IF YOU CAPTURE THE OTHER GUY'S FLAG AND MAKE IT BACK TO YOUR TERRITORY, YOU WIN.
WIN WHAT?
THE GAME.
NO LUGGAGE? NO TOASTER OVEN?
HEY, YOU CAN'T HIDE YOUR FLAG IN A TREE! IT'S TOO HARD TO CAPTURE!
THAT'S NOT A RULE. I CAN HIDE MY FLAG ANYWHERE!
WELL, IT'S A RULE NOW! FROM NOW ON, NO FLAGS IN TREES!
OK, BUT I JUST TAGGED YOU, SO YOU HAVE TO GO TO JAIL.
WHAT?!? IT'S A TIME OUT! I WAS MAKING A NEW RULE!
YOU DIDN'T OFFICIALLY CALL A TIME OUT. OFF TO JAIL WITH YOU!
FORGET IT! FROM NOW ON, IF YOU'RE DISCUSSING A NEW RULE, IT'S AUTOMATICALLY A TIME OUT.
OK, TIME IN!
TAG!
YOU CAN'T DO THAT! WE HAVE TO SAY "TIME IN" TOGETHER!
SINCE WHEN?? YOU'RE JUST CHANGING THE RULES SO YOU'LL WIN!
I AM NOT! I'M JUST TRYING TO KEEP YOU FROM CHEATING!
JUST A MINUTE, MUFFIN HEAD. ARE YOU CALLING ME A CHEATER?
WHO'S A MUFFIN HEAD?
STRUDEL BRAIN!
YOWP!
OATMEAL FACE!
ARRGH
MOM SAYS WE SHOULD TAKE UP MONOPOLY.
NO WAY, BUSTER. I KNOW ALL ABOUT THOSE "INTEREST-FREE BANK LOANS" TO YOURSELF!
WATTERSON

LOOK, MOM, I PUT ALL MY CLOTHES FOR TOMORROW ON THE STAIRS.
THEN IN THE MORNING, I'LL RUN OUT IN MY UNDERWEAR AND SLIDE DOWN AT TOP SPEED!
IF I AIM GOOD, I GO RIGHT INTO MY PANTS WHILE I'M PUTTING ON MY SHIRT, AND BY THE BOTTOM, I'M ALL DRESSED FOR SCHOOL!
WATTERSON
AND IF YOU PUT MY CEREAL ON THE STAIRS TOO, I WON'T HAVE TO GET UP UNTIL 30 SECONDS BEFORE THE BUS COMES.
FORGET IT, CALVIN.

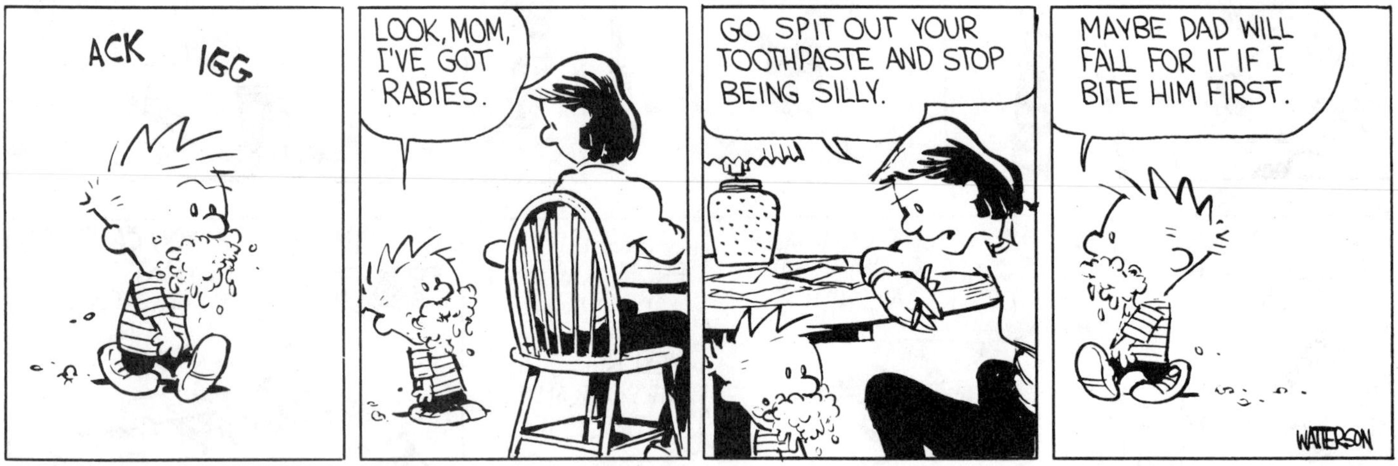
ACK
IGG
LOOK, MOM, I'VE GOT RABIES.
GO SPIT OUT YOUR TOOTHPASTE AND STOP BEING SILLY.
MAYBE DAD WILL FALL FOR IT IF I BITE HIM FIRST.
WATTERSON

WHAT ARE YOU GOING TO DRESS UP AS FOR HALLOWEEN?
I DON'T KNOW YET. I CAN'T DECIDE.
WATTERSON
WELL, THE IDEA IS TO BE THE SCARIEST THING YOU CAN THINK OF.
HMM...MAYBE I'LL JUST GO AS MYSELF!
I'M GOING AS A BARREL OF TOXIC WASTE!

WE'RE GOING TO CARVE A JACK-O'-LANTERN NOW.
SEE, WE'LL MAKE A FACE ON THIS PUMPKIN SO IT WILL LOOK LIKE A HEAD.
BUT FIRST WE HAVE TO OPEN UP THE TOP AND SCOOP OUT THE GLOP INSIDE.
OK, JACK, TIME FOR YOUR LOBOTOMY!!
HAND ME A BIG SPOON, WILL YOU, HOBBES?
UGH! NO ANESTHETIC EVEN.
WATTERSON

I THINK DAD LIKES HALLOWEEN AS MUCH AS WE DO.
IS HE TAKING US TRICK OR TREATING TONIGHT?
NO, MOM IS.
IS HE GOING TO STAY HOME AND GIVE OUT CANDY?
NO, HE'S GOING TO SIT IN THE BUSHES WITH THE GARDEN HOSE AND DRENCH POTENTIAL T.P.ERS.
WATTERSON

OOG, I FEEL AWFUL.
IF SOMEONE EVEN MENTIONS "MILK DUDS," I'M GONNA BARF.
ANOTHER HALLOWEEN COME AND GONE.
IT'S ALWAYS SUCH A LETDOWN AFTER A HOLIDAY.
WE MIGHT AS WELL GO INTO TOWN AND LOOK AT THE CHRISTMAS DECORATIONS.
WATTERSON

Calvin and HOBBES
by WATTERSON
RED ALERT!
ENEMY SIGHTED! BATTLE STATIONS! BATTLE STATIONS!
AHWOOGA! AHWOOGA!
HERE'S THE MIGHTY AIRCRAFT CARRIER!
EQUIPPED WITH THE LATEST IN RADAR AND FIREPOWER, IT IS VIRTUALLY UNSINKABLE!
I KNOW WHAT CAN SINK IT.
YEAH? WHAT?
A CANNONBALL DEPTH CHARGE!!
OH NO!
PFOOM!
HA HA! THAT WAS GREAT! YOU EMPTIED THE WHOLE TUB! TURN ON THE WATER AND LET'S DO IT AGAIN!
WATTERSON
WE SEEM TO HAVE A WATERFALL DOWN THE STAIRWAY, DEAR. I'LL GO SEE WHAT YOUR KID IS DOING.
MY KID?!? C'MERE AND LET ME EXPLAIN SOMETHING TO YOU...

MOM'S NOT FEELING WELL, SO I'M MAKING HER A "GET WELL" CARD.
THAT'S THOUGHTFUL OF YOU.
SEE, ON THE FRONT IT SAYS, "GET WELL SOON."
AND ON THE INSIDE IT SAYS, "BECAUSE MY BED ISN'T MADE, MY CLOTHES NEED TO BE PUT AWAY, AND I'M HUNGRY."
"LOVE, CALVIN." WANT TO SIGN IT?
SURE. I'M HUNGRY TOO.
WATTERSON

HI, MOM! SINCE YOU'RE SICK, I'M BRINGING YOU BREAKFAST IN BED!
I PREPARED EGGS, TOAST AND ORANGE JUICE FOR YOU ALL BY MYSELF!
HOW NICE!
THE EGGS KIND OF BURNED AND STUCK TO THE PAN, BUT YOU CAN PROBABLY CHIP THEM OUT WITH THIS CHISEL.
UM... WHERE IS THE TOAST AND ORANGE JUICE?
DAD SAID NOT TO TELL YOU ABOUT THAT TILL YOU'RE BETTER.
WATTERSON

SINCE YOUR MOM'S SICK, I'LL BE MAKING DINNER TONIGHT.
YOU CAN COOK?
OF COURSE I CAN COOK.
WATTERSON
AS YOU CAN SEE, I SURVIVED TWO YEARS OF MY OWN COOKING WHEN I HAD AN APARTMENT AFTER COLLEGE.
MOM SAYS YOU ATE FROZEN WAFFLES AND CANNED SOUP THREE MEALS A DAY.
YOUR MOM WASN'T THERE, SO SHE WOULDN'T KNOW. GET THE SYRUP OUT, WILL YOU?

SOMETIMES WHEN *I'M* SICK, YOU READ ME A STORY. WANT ME TO READ *YOU* ONE?
NO, THANKS, CALVIN. I JUST WANT TO REST.
WATERSON
IT'S HARD TO BE A MOM FOR A MOM.
YOU DO FINE, SWEETIE.
WHOA! HEY! ARE YOU CONTAGIOUS?!

WHAT'S WRONG WITH YOUR MOM, DO YOU KNOW?
NO. SHE WENT TO THE DOCTOR TODAY, THOUGH.
I WONDER IF... NAH.
WHAT?
WATERSON
YOU DON'T SUPPOSE SHE'S GOING TO HAVE A BABY, DO YOU?
A BABY?!
WHY WOULD SHE WANT ANOTHER KID?? SHE'S ALREADY GOT *ME!*
YES, YOU'D THINK SHE'D HAVE LEARNED HER LESSON...

I ASKED DAD IF MOM WAS GOING TO HAVE A BABY, AND HE SAID NOT THAT *HE* KNEW OF.
DAD SAID WE'D KNOW IF MOM WAS HAVING A KID BECAUSE SHE'D LOOK LIKE A HIPPOPOTAMUS WITH A GLAND PROBLEM.
...THAT'S WHEN MOM CREAMED HIM WITH HER PILLOW.
DAD SAYS SHE MUST BE FEELING BETTER.
YOU HAVE WEIRD PARENTS.
WATERSON

Calvin and Hobbes
by WATTERSON
BANG!
KAPWINNGG!
BANG BANG
YOU MISSED! YOU MISSED!
THERE HE GOES! AFTER HIM, BOYS!
GIDDYAP! GIDDYAP!
BONK!
BONK!
AMBUSH! BANG! BANG!
YOW! WHOOP!
BANG! GOTCHA!
NOYADINT! NOYADINT!
CALVIN, WILL YOU PLEASE STOP TEARING AROUND THE HOUSE?! YOU'RE DRIVING ME CRAZY!
YOU SAID WE COULDN'T GO OUTSIDE BECAUSE IT'S RAINING.
BOY, THAT SURE WORKED.
WE'RE NOT ALLOWED BACK IN UNTIL WHEN?
WATTERSON

HEY, MOM, I GOT A PART IN THE CLASS PLAY!
I GET TO SAY A LINE, AND EVERYTHING!
THAT'S WONDERFUL, CALVIN.
IT'S A GREAT DRAMATIC ROLE! MY CHARACTER WILL HAVE EVERYONE IN TEARS AT THE END OF THE SECOND ACT!
WHAT'S THE PLAY?
"NUTRITION AND THE FOUR FOOD GROUPS." I'M AN ONION.

OK, HOBBES, I NEED YOU TO HELP ME MEMORIZE MY LINE FOR THE PLAY.
SURE.
I'M THE ONION, AND I SAY, "IN ADDITION TO SUPPLYING VITAL NUTRIENTS, MANY VEGETABLES ARE A SOURCE OF DIETARY FIBER."
OK, READY?
READY. GO AHEAD. "IN ADDITION..."
WAIT. HOLD IT. I'M NOT IN CHARACTER YET. WHAT MOTIVATES AN ONION?
FAME, I SUPPOSE. THIS COULD BE A BIG BREAK.

OK, YOU BE "BREAD." PROMPT ME.
"GLUCOSE IS THE BODY'S MAIN ENERGY SOURCE!"
"IN ADDITION..." UH... UM... "IN ADDITION.." UM... WAIT..
GRRRGHH! I HATE THIS PLAY! I'LL NEVER BE ABLE TO LEARN THIS STUPID PART!
WELL, YOUR EMOTING IS DOWN PAT.

I'VE GOT IT ALL FIGURED OUT, HOBBES. THIS PLAY WILL BE NO SWEAT.
YOU HAVE YOUR LINE ALL MEMORIZED?
NO, I THOUGHT I'D COME OUT, DO A LITTLE SOFT-SHOE, AND AD-LIB SOMETHING!
AD-LIB SOMETHING ABOUT DIETARY FIBER?
EITHER THAT, OR I'LL DO MY ONION IN MIME!
WATTERSON

HOW'S MY ONION COSTUME COMING, MOM?
I'M STILL WORKING ON IT. I WISH YOUR CLASS WOULD DO SOMETHING A LITTLE LESS ELABORATE. I'M NOT MUCH OF A SEAMSTRESS.
JUST BE GLAD I'M NOT RUSSY WHITE. HE HAS TO BE AN AMINO ACID.
MM... WHAT DO YOU THINK?
JABBA THE HUTT MEETS RUDOLF THE REINDEER. I DUNNO, MOM.
WATTERSON

ARE YOU GOING TO COME TO MY PLAY, DAD? IT'S CALLED "NUTRITION AND THE FOUR FOOD GROUPS."
WATTERSON
I'LL PROBABLY HAVE TO BE AT WORK, CALVIN.
BUT DAD, IT'LL BE GREAT DRAMA! I'M AN ONION!
WELL, WHY DON'T YOU SAY YOUR LINE FOR ME NOW?
OK! UM... ..LET'S SEE.. "IN ADDITION TO..." .. UH... HOLD IT... UM..
25 KIDS IN FOOD SUITS, FORGETTING THEIR LINES. I'LL DEFINITELY BE AT WORK.
DEAR! CALVIN'S WORKED HARD.
OK, UH... "IN ADDITION.."..UH NO, WAIT.. UM...

DO YOU HAVE YOUR LINE MEMORIZED FOR THE NUTRITION PLAY, CALVIN?
I'M STILL LEARNING IT. BEING AN ONION IS A DIFFICULT ROLE, YOU KNOW. WHAT ARE YOU?
I'M "FAT."
NO, I MEAN IN THE PLAY.
ANYONE *ELSE* WANT TO SAY IT ?!?
AACKK! UNDERSTUDY! UNDERSTUDY!
WATTERSON

THANKS FOR WAITING FOR THE BUS WITH ME, HOBBES. I FEEL LIKE AN IDIOT IN THIS ONION SUIT.
I'LL BE GLAD WHEN THIS STUPID PLAY IS OVER.
OH NO! RUN FOR YOUR LIFE! A PRODUCE TRUCK!
...JUST KIDDING!
WATTERSON

SUSIE, WHERE'S CALVIN? HE GOES ONSTAGE RIGHT AFTER YOU!
I DON'T KNOW, MISS WORMWOOD. HE WAS HERE A MINUTE AGO.
MAYBE HE WENT TO THE BOYS' ROOM.
HE'S ON IN TWO MINUTES! FINE TIME TO GO TO THE BOYS' ROOM!
FINE TIME TO GET STUCK IN MY COSTUME. STUPID ZIPPER!
WATTERSON

I CAN'T BELIEVE IT! I'M STUCK IN MY ONION SUIT!
I CAN'T GO ONSTAGE WITH MY SHIRT CAUGHT IN MY COSTUME! HELP! HELP!
I'M SUPPOSED TO BE ON NOW! I'M SUPPOSED TO BE SAYING MY LINE! WHAT SHOULD I DO?? WHAT SHOULD I DO??
"IN ADDITION TO SUPPLYING VITAL NUTRIENTS, MANY VEGETABLES ARE A SOURCE OF DIETARY FIBER!!"
WATTERSON

I'M HOME!
HI, HONEY. HOW DID YOUR PLAY GO?
TERRIBLE. I GOT STUCK IN MY ZIPPER IN THE BATHROOM, AND THEY HAD TO STOP THE PLAY AND GET A JANITOR TO FIND ME AND GET ME OUT.
OH NO. THAT'S AWFUL!
I'LL SAY... THE PLAY WAS RUINED.
...BUT I REMEMBERED MY LINE!
WATTERSON

UP, UP AND AWAY!
WOOMPH!
ACKK! KRYPTONITE! KRYPTONITE!
WATTERSON

Calvin and HOBBES by WATTERSON
ZIP ZOP ZIP ZOP ZIP ZOP ZIP ZOP ZIP ZOP ZIP ZOP
SNOW PANTS.
WELL? LET'S HAVE SOME SNOW!!
IT'S SNOWING! I CAN MAKE IT SNOW! I'M PSYCHOKINETIC! HEY! HEY!
OOH, HE'S GOING TO HATE ME FOR THIS.
WATTERSON

WANT TO TRADE SANDWICHES, CALVIN?
NO, I'VE GOT MY FAVORITE KIND. WHAT DID YOU BRING?
WATTERSON
PEANUT BUTTER.
I HAVE PROCESSED MOUSE LOAF.
OH, GROSS. THAT'S NOT REALLY MOUSE LOAF. IT LOOKS LIKE EGG SALAD.
TASTE IT AND SEE. HERE, I THINK THIS IS A WHISKER. IT'S GOOD.
FORGET IT. I DON'T EVEN WANT MY OWN LUNCH ANY MORE.
YOU DON'T? WHAT KIND OF COOKIES ARE THOSE?

TRIP!
TA-DAAA!!
WATTERSON

HOW DO THEY KNOW THE LOAD LIMIT ON BRIDGES, DAD?
LOAD LIMIT 10 TONS
THEY DRIVE BIGGER AND BIGGER TRUCKS OVER THE BRIDGE UNTIL IT BREAKS.
THEN THEY WEIGH THE LAST TRUCK AND REBUILD THE BRIDGE.
WATTERSON
OH. I SHOULD'VE GUESSED.
DEAR, IF YOU DON'T KNOW THE ANSWER, JUST TELL HIM!

IT'S HARD TO BELIEVE PEOPLE STILL STARVE IN THIS WORLD.
THERE'S EVEN HUNGER IN AMERICA.
SOME PEOPLE NEVER GET ENOUGH TO EAT.
BOY, I KNOW WHAT **THAT'S** LIKE!
NO YOU DON'T.
WATTERSON

THE SOLDIERS ADVANCE UP THE HILL!
OH, NO! A SQUADRON OF BOMBERS APPEARS ON THE HORIZON! THE BOMBS BEGIN TO FALL!
BONK
BONK
TWO DIRECT HITS!
I SEE YOU UP THERE!
WATTERSON

LOOK, HOBBES, YOU GET A PLASTIC TRINKET IN BOXES OF "CHOCOLATE-FROSTED SUGAR BOMBS"!
IT SAYS, "BE THE FIRST IN YOUR NEIGHBORHOOD TO COLLECT ALL TEN COLORS."
YEAH, BUT MOM SAYS SHE WON'T BUY ANY MORE CEREAL UNTIL THIS BOX IS GONE.
THAT SHOULDN'T TAKE MORE THAN A COUPLE HOURS, RIGHT?
I DUNNO. AFTER FIVE BOWLS, I GET PRETTY WIRED.
WATTERSON

Calvin and HOBBES
by WATTERSON
CAN HOBBES AND I COME IN THE STORE WITH YOU, DAD?
NO, YOU STAY IN THE CAR.
SHEESH. KNOCK OVER ONE LOUSY DISPLAY STAND, AND PAY FOR IT THE REST OF YOUR LIFE.
I'LL JUST BE A MINUTE. WAIT HERE.
OK.
LET'S HIDE AND GIVE DAD A SCARE! MAYBE HE'LL THINK WE RAN AWAY!
HEE HEE!
LIE DOWN AND I'LL PULL THIS BLANKET OVER US.
THEN PUT THIS BAG ON TOP.
HEE HEE! I HEAR HIM COMING!
SSHHH! HEE HEE!
GEE, I WONDER WHERE CALVIN WENT! AND HIS TIGER'S GONE TOO!
HEE HEE!! MPH. SHHH!
NOW'S MY CHANCE TO GET AWAY BEFORE THEY GET BACK! WON'T MOM BE GLAD WHEN SHE HEARS I LOST THEM!
!!
MOM WON'T BE GLAD AT ALL, YOU SICKO! SORRY TO SPOIL YOUR GETAWAY!
WHAT? YOU'RE HERE?? OH RATS...I MEAN, GOOD!
WATTERSON

CALVIN, YOUR DAD AND I ARE GOING OUT TOMORROW, SO YOU'LL BE HAVING A BABY SITTER.
OH NO! NOT ROSALYN!
I CALLED EIGHT PEOPLE AND SHE'S THE ONLY ONE WHO WOULD DO IT.
CALL SOME MORE! CALL SOME MORE!
CALVIN, I SPENT AN HOUR ON THE PHONE ALREADY. ROSALYN'S FINE.
"FINE"?? SHE'S A BARRACUDA IN A HIGH SCHOOL SENIOR SUIT! I'M AS GOOD AS DEAD!
YOU REMEMBER AMY? SHE JUST LAUGHED WHEN I CALLED HER.
WATTERSON

OH NO! A KNOCK AT THE DOOR! THE BABY SITTER MUST BE HERE!
SHOULD WE HIDE?
NO WAY. BABY SITTERS CAN SMELL FEAR IN LITTLE KIDS. WE'D BE DOOMED.
SO WE GO ON THE OFFENSIVE?
RIGHT. HERE'S A NOTEPAD AND PENCIL.
OH BOY, BLACKMAIL!
RIGHT. GET TO THE UPSTAIRS PHONE WHEN SHE CALLS HER BOYFRIEND.
WATTERSON

WE'RE GOING, ROSALYN. HELP YOURSELF TO ANYTHING IN THE FRIDGE.
OK, GOOD-BYE.
CALVIN? ARE YOU UPSTAIRS?
WAP
WAP
ALL RIGHT, KID! BEDTIME FOR BONZO!!
WHAT?! GET AWAY! IT'S NOT EVEN 6 O'CLOCK!
WATTERSON

I CAN'T BELIEVE OUR BABY SITTER PUT US TO BED! IT'S NOT EVEN DARK OUT!
WELL, SHE CAN PUT US TO BED, BUT SHE CAN'T MAKE US SLEEP. YOU PLAY THE HORN, AND I'LL ACCOMPANY ON TOM-TOM.
CALVIN, I JUST WANTED TO REMIND YOU THAT SLEEPING IN A BED IS A PRIVILEGE. THE BASEMENT IS SURE TO BE A LOT LESS COMFY.
WHAT DID SHE MEAN, "THE BASEMENT"?
SHHH!
WATTERSON

ROSALYN, WE'RE GOING TO BE A LITTLE LATER THAN WE EXPECTED, SO I THOUGHT I'D BETTER CALL YOU.
THAT'S FINE. CALVIN WENT TO BED EARLY, SO I'M JUST HOLDING DOWN THE FORT.
WHO'S ON THE PHONE? IS IT MY MOM? I WANT TO TALK TO HER! MOM! MOM! CAN YOU HEAR ME?!
COME HOME NOW BEFORE IT'S TOO LATE! HELP! HELP!
NO, THAT'S JUST THE TV. I'LL SEE YOU AT 11:30 THEN. ENJOY THE PLAY.
WATTERSON

SORRY WE'RE LATE, ROSALYN. DID YOU GET CALVIN TO BED?
YES, BUT...
MOM! DAD! IS THAT YOU? I'M NOT ASLEEP! DID YOU GET RID OF THE BABY SITTER? THANK GOODNESS YOU'RE HOME!
HAS HE BEEN THIS WAY ALL NIGHT?
WELL, HIS VOICE GAVE OUT ABOUT 11 O'CLOCK, BUT IT SEEMS TO BE...
WATTERSON
IF SHE'S STILL HERE, DON'T PAY HER!
GIVE HER A LITTLE EXTRA, WILL YOU, DEAR?
IS FIVE ENOUGH?
COULD YOU MAKE IT EIGHT? COLLEGE TUITIONS ARE UP.

Calvin and HOBBES
by WATTERSON
A BRILLIANT BOLT OF DEADLY FRAP RAY BLAZES BY THE INTREPID SPACEMAN SPIFF!
OUR HERO HAS VERY HIGH INSURANCE PREMIUMS.
THE COURAGEOUS SPACEMAN SPIFF IS HIT! HE PLUMMETS TOWARD PLANET ZOG!
BREAKING THROUGH THE CLOUD LAYER, HE CAREENS OVER AN ALIEN CITY! THERE'S NO PLACE TO LAND!
SPIFF WRESTLES THE UNCOOPERATIVE CONTROLS! MORE FREEM DRIVE TO THE THRUSTER BLASTERS!
TOO MUCH STRESS! THE FUEL EXPLODES IN FLAME!
THE SITUATION IS GRIM! TEN SECONDS TO IMPACT! NINE .... EIGHT...
WELL, CALVIN??
SEVEN!
VERY GOOD, CALVIN. TEN MINUS THREE EQUALS SEVEN. I DIDN'T THINK YOU WERE PAYING ATTENTION. THAT QUESTION WAS WORTH THREE POINTS.
OUR HERO MIRACULOUSLY MAKES A THREE-POINT LANDING. SPIFF SAVES THE DAY AGAIN!
WATTERSON

WHAT A ROTTEN DAY.
ZZ...MMP.. BGZ..
AHHHH...
GNZ.. HEE HEE ZZZ..
FUZZ THERAPY.
ZZZ.. NUK NUK WOONK..
WATTERSON

HELLO SUSIE, THIS IS CALVIN. I LOST OUR HOMEWORK ASSIGNMENT. CAN YOU TELL ME WHAT WE WERE SUPPOSED TO READ FOR TOMORROW?
ARE YOU SURE YOU'RE NOT CALLING FOR SOME OTHER REASON?
WHY ELSE WOULD I CALL YOU?
MAYBE YOU MISSED THE MELODIOUS SOUND OF MY VOICE.
WHAT ARE YOU, CRAZY?? ALL I WANT IS THE STUPID ASSIGNMENT!
FIRST SAY YOU MISSED THE MELODIOUS SOUND OF MY VOICE.
THIS IS BLACKMAIL!
WATTERSON

I'M HOME FROM SCHOOL!
OOF!
HELLOO
BONK
BING
BOING
HOW'S THAT FOR AN ENTHUSIASTIC GREETING??
SOMETIMES I WISH YOU'D JUST BUY ME ONE OF THOSE "I MISSED YOU" CARDS.
WATTERSON

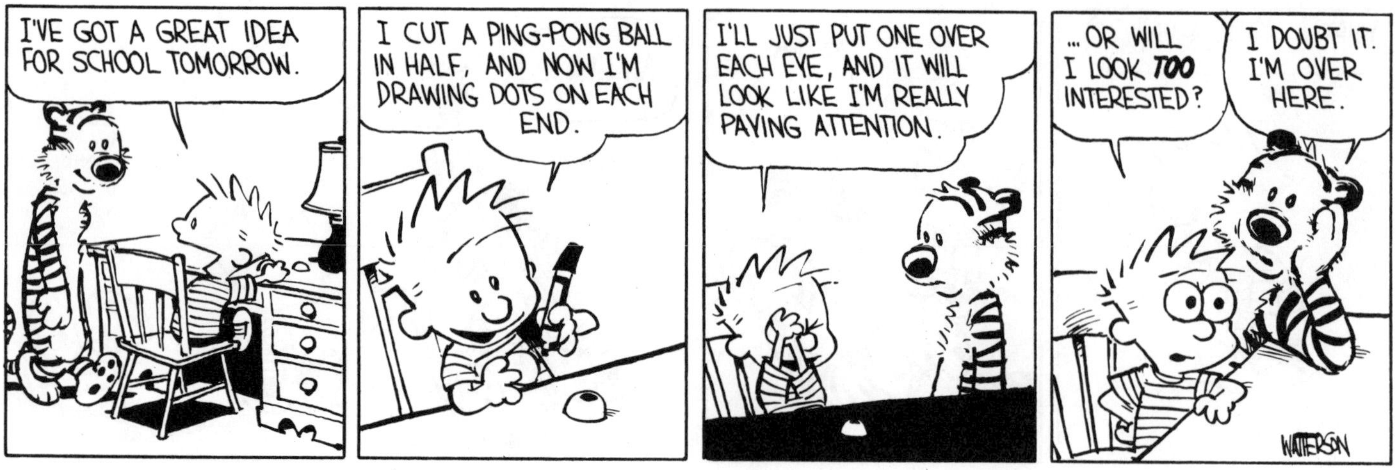
I'VE GOT A GREAT IDEA FOR SCHOOL TOMORROW.
I CUT A PING-PONG BALL IN HALF, AND NOW I'M DRAWING DOTS ON EACH END.
I'LL JUST PUT ONE OVER EACH EYE, AND IT WILL LOOK LIKE I'M REALLY PAYING ATTENTION.
...OR WILL I LOOK TOO INTERESTED?
I DOUBT IT. I'M OVER HERE.
WATTERSON

BAD NEWS ON YOUR POLLS, DAD.
YOU SLIPPED ANOTHER TWO NOTCHES. THINGS ARE LOOKING GRIM FOR FUTURE OFFICE.
IS THAT SO?
ANY IDEAS ON WHAT WOULD IMPROVE MY STANDINGS?
I NEED A VCR.
RIGHT. I'LL KEEP THAT IN MIND.
I HOPE YOU'RE READING THE "HELP WANTED" SECTION.
WATTERSON

LOOK, I GOT A LETTER I'M SUPPOSED TO COPY AND SEND TO 20 PEOPLE FOR GOOD LUCK.
IT'S A CHAIN LETTER.
WATTERSON
IT SAYS, "A MAN IN DENVER MADE 20 COPIES AND THE NEXT DAY HE GOT A RAISE. A MAN IN SEATTLE BROKE THE CHAIN AND HE WENT BALD."
HA! YOU BELIEVE THAT? THESE LETTERS ARE FOR SUPERSTITIOUS NINCOMPOOPS. THROW IT AWAY.
"...AND A DUMB KID LIKE YOU LISTENED TO A FRIEND AND GOT RUN OVER BY A CEMENT MIXER."

Calvin and Hobbes
by WATTERSON
I'M READY FOR BED, DAD. WHAT'S TONIGHT'S STORY GOING TO BE?
HERE'S ONE. "READINGS ON DIALECTICAL METAPHYSICS." YOU'LL LOVE IT.
FORGET IT, DAD. YOU CAN'T GET ME TO DROP OFF THAT EASY.
WILL YOU READ US THIS STORY? HOBBES WROTE IT HIMSELF.
HOBBES WROTE IT, HUH?
"GOLDILOCKS AND THE THREE TIGERS."
OH BOY, THIS IS GONNA BE GREAT!
"ONCE UPON A TIME THERE LIVED A YOUNG GIRL NAMED GOLDILOCKS. SHE WENT INTO THE FOREST AND SAW A COTTAGE. NO ONE WAS HOME SO SHE WENT IN."
"INSIDE SHE SAW THREE BOWLS OF PORRIDGE. A BIG BOWL, A MEDIUM BOWL, AND A SMALL BOWL. SHE WAS JUST ABOUT TO TASTE THE PORRIDGE WHEN THE THREE TIGERS CAME HOME."
"THEY QUICKLY DIVIDED GOLDILOCKS INTO BIG, MEDIUM, AND SMALL PIECES AND DUNKED THEM IN THE PORRIDGE THAT..."
CALVIN, I'M NOT GOING TO FINISH THIS! THIS IS DISGUSTING!!
I DON'T KNOW WHY I LET YOU TALK ME INTO THIS. GOOD NIGHT!
CLICK
WATTERSON
HE DIDN'T EVEN LOOK AT OUR ILLUSTRATIONS.
NOW I'M ALL HUNGRY.

Calvin and HOBBES
by WATTERSON
UM.. 2 POINTS.
I SPELLED "BE." HOW MANY POINTS DO I GET?
2 POINTS?! IS THAT @*#%! ALL?!?
MY, THIS GAME DOES TEACH NEW WORDS!
SEE, I SPELLED "ZYGOMORPHIC" ON A TRIPLE WORD SCORE BOX. THAT'S 150 POINTS.
ALL I'VE GOT IS CONSONANTS.
YOUR TURN.
WELL, IF I USE YOUR LETTER "I", I CAN SPELL "IN." THAT'S 3 POINTS.
I PICK OUT SOME NEW LETTERS... HMM... WITH YOUR "N", I CAN SPELL "NUCLEOPLASM." THAT'S, LET'S SEE, 40 POINTS.
ALL I'VE GOT IS CONSONANTS.
I'M NOT GOING TO PLAY THIS STUPID GAME! I HATE IT!! WHAT A WASTE OF TIME!
WHAT SHOULD WE PLAY INSTEAD?
LET'S PLAY POKER. AT LEAST WITH CARDS YOU HAVE HALF A CHANCE.
OK, I BET A NICKEL.
I'LL SEE YOU .. AND RAISE YOU 8 DOLLARS.
WATTERSON

CALVIN HAS MYSTERIOUSLY SHRUNK TO THE SIZE OF AN INSECT!
HIS ONLY HOPE IS TO CALL FOR HELP! PUSHING WITH ALL HIS MIGHT, CALVIN DIALS THE GIGANTIC TELEPHONE!
DEF 3
ABC 2
1
IT'S RINGING! HE RUNS TO THE MOUTHPIECE! WILL ANYONE BE ABLE TO HEAR HIM??
BZZ BZ! BZZZZ! BZZ BZZ! BZZZ BZ!
CALVIN, THIS HAD BETTER NOT BE YOU.
WATTERSON

FWOOSHHH
WATTERSON
GREETINGS, EARTH FEMALE. DO NOT BE ALARMED.
OUR PLANET IS DYING. WE NEED COOKIES TO SURVIVE. DO NOT TRY TO RESIST OR YOU WILL BE DESTROYED.
WE'LL SEE ABOUT THAT. GET BACK HERE.

WHY DO I HAVE TO GO TO BED NOW? I NEVER GET TO DO WHAT I WANT!
IF I GROW UP TO BE SOME SORT OF PSYCHOPATH BECAUSE OF THIS, YOU'LL ALL BE SORRY!!
WATTERSON
NOBODY EVER BECAME A PSYCHOPATH BECAUSE HE HAD TO GO TO BED AT A REASONABLE HOUR.
YEAH, BUT YOU WON'T LET ME CHEW TOBACCO EITHER! YOU NEVER KNOW WHAT MIGHT PUSH ME OVER THE BRINK!
GO TO BED, CALVIN.

THIS OUIJA BOARD KNOWS ALL AND TELLS ALL.
WHAT SHOULD WE ASK IT?
LET'S ASK IT WHICH OF US IS SMARTER.
OK, GO AHEAD.
OH GREAT OUIJA BOARD, WHO IS SMARTER, CALVIN OR HOBBES?
QUIT RESISTING, YOU! IT'S HEADING FOR THE "H"!
HA! IT'S OBVIOUSLY **TRYING** TO (MMF) GO TO "C," YOU CHEATER!

LET'S ASK THE OUIJA BOARD ANOTHER QUESTION.
OK, I'VE GOT ONE.
OH GREAT OUIJA BOARD, WILL I GROW UP TO BE PRESIDENT?
IT'S MOVING!
"G...O..."
"D..F...O... R... B... I... D."
WHEN I WANT AN EDITORIAL, I'LL **ASK** FOR IT, YOU STUPID BOARD!

HOW IS IT THAT THIS OUIJA BOARD KNOWS ALL THE ANSWERS TO LIFE'S MYSTERIES?
LET'S ASK IT.
OH GREAT OUIJA BOARD, HOW DO YOU KNOW ALL THE ANSWERS?
IT'S MOVING! IT'S MOVING!
WHAT'S IT SAY?
"3."
YOU KNOW, I DIDN'T ASK FOR THIS LAST CHRISTMAS. I ASKED FOR A COMPUTER.

Calvin and Hobbes
by WATTERSON
RUN!
AIEEE!
LOOK OUT!
I WONDER WHY JAPANESE PEOPLE KEEP MOVING THEIR MOUTHS AFTER THEY'RE THROUGH TALKING.
SOMEWHERE IN THE PACIFIC OCEAN...
AN UNDERSEA NUCLEAR EXPLOSION AWAKENS A GIANT PREHISTORIC MONSTER!
IT MAKES ITS WAY TO THE COAST OF JAPAN AND EMERGES!
YAARGHHH
WATTERSON
HE HEADS FOR THE POWER LINES, LEAVING A TRAIL OF DESTRUCTION BEHIND!
CALVIN, GET BACK IN THE TUB! YOU'RE MAKING A MESS!
HIS ANCIENT ARCH-RIVAL MEGALON!
HE SPEWS A MIGHTY FIREBALL!
AAUUGHH
TOKYO IS IN RUINS! MEGALON VANQUISHED! HE RETURNS TO THE SEA FROM WHENCE HE CAME!
NO MORE AFTERNOON TV MOVIES FOR YOU! ..EVER!!

OH BOY, YOU GOT SOME CLAY.
I'M MAKING MOM AND DAD A CHRISTMAS PRESENT.
WHAT ARE YOU MAKING?
AN ASHTRAY.
YOUR PARENTS DON'T SMOKE, OF COURSE...
OK, MICHELANGELO, YOU SCULPT SOMETHING!
WATTERSON

A HOMEMADE GIFT SAYS MORE THAN A STORE-BOUGHT GIFT.
IT SAYS YOU CARE ENOUGH TO INVEST YOUR TIME AND SKILL IN IT.
IT SAYS THIS IS A PERSONAL GIFT, NOT A GENERIC ONE.
IT SAYS YOU NEED A BIGGER ALLOWANCE.
WATTERSON

THIS ARTICLE SAYS THAT MANY PEOPLE FIND CHRISTMAS THE MOST STRESSFUL TIME OF YEAR.
I BELIEVE IT. THIS SEASON SURE FILLS ME WITH STRESS.
REALLY? HOW COME?
I HATE BEING GOOD.
WATTERSON

PSST! ARE YOU AWAKE?
IS IT CHRISTMAS? IT IS! IT IS!
LET'S GO WAKE MOM AND DAD AND OPEN ALL OUR LOOT!
SINCE IT'S CHRISTMAS, MAYBE WE SHOULD LET THEM SLEEP IN A LITTLE.
WATTERSON
THAT'S LONG ENOUGH! WAKE UP! WAKE UP! IT'S CHRISTMAS!!
QUARTER TO 6. HE LET US SLEEP IN THIS YEAR.

OMIGOSH! THIS LIBRARY BOOK WAS DUE TWO DAYS AGO!
WHAT WILL THEY DO? ARE THEY GOING TO INTERROGATE ME AND BEAT ME UP?! ARE THEY GOING TO BREAK MY KNEES?? WILL I HAVE TO SIGN SOME CONFESSION???
THEY'LL FINE YOU TEN CENTS. NOW GO RETURN IT.
THE WAY SOME OF THOSE LIBRARIANS LOOK AT YOU, I NATURALLY ASSUMED THE CONSEQUENCES WOULD BE MORE DIRE.
WATTERSON

HEY DAD, I HAVE A QUESTION.
SURE, CALVIN. WHAT DO YOU WANT TO KNOW?
WATTERSON
IF YOU PLUGGED UP YOUR NOSE AND MOUTH RIGHT BEFORE YOU SNEEZED...
...WOULD THE SNEEZE GO OUT YOUR EARS, OR WOULD YOUR HEAD EXPLODE?
I WAS KIND OF HOPING YOU HAD A MATH PROBLEM OR SOMETHING.
...EITHER WAY, I'M SCARED TO TRY IT.

Calvin and HobbEs
by WATTERSON
TOBOGGANS GIVE BETTER RIDES THAN RUNNER SLEDS.
WHY IS THAT?
THERE'S NO WAY TO STEER.
ON THESE CLOUDY WINTER DAYS, SOMETIMES I LIKE TO LIE BACK ON MY SLED AND LOOK AT THE SKY.
IT'S JUST GRAY AND SILENT. NO BIRDS SINGING OR BUGS BUZZING. EVERYTHING IS MUFFLED BY THE SNOW.
IMAGINE WHAT IT WOULD BE LIKE WITHOUT ANY PEOPLE OR HOUSES AROUND. IT WOULD BE PERFECTLY STILL.
WATTERSON
PRETTY NEAT, HUH?
YES, VERY PEACEFUL.
AAAAAAAAAAAAAAAAAAAAAAAAHH
I HATE ALL THAT SILENCE.

BEHOLD THE DREADED TOBOGGAN: SUICIDE SLED.
ITS UNIQUE DESIGN SENDS A BLINDING SPRAY OF SNOW ON ITS PASSENGERS AT THE SLIGHTEST BUMP. NOTE, TOO, THE LACK OF ANY STEERING MECHANISM.
YES, THIS SLED IS TRULY A HAZARD TO LIFE AND LIMB.
WHEEE OOMPH! EEEEE
WATTERSON

BOY, IS IT COLD! CAN'T WE TURN THE HEAT UP?
HEAT IS EXPENSIVE, CALVIN. JUST PUT ON A SWEATER.
LOOK, THE THERMOSTAT GOES ALL THE WAY UP TO 90 DEGREES! WE COULD BE SITTING AROUND IN OUR SHORTS!
LEAVE THE THERMOSTAT ALONE, CALVIN.
I CAN ALMOST SEE MY BREATH. I'LL JUST CRANK IT UP TO 75, OK?
I SAID DON'T TOUCH IT!
GEE, MY HANDS ARE SO NUMB, I CAN'T MOVE THE SWITCH. GUESS I'LL PUT ON A SWEATER.
WATTERSON

OOH, YOU LOOK COLD, CALVIN! THERE'S A FIRE MADE. WHY DON'T YOU GO WARM UP?
OH BOY!
NOTHING BEATS SITTING BY A ROARING FIRE AFTER YOU'VE BEEN OUT IN THE COLD.
WATTERSON
OF COURSE, SOME PEOPLE SAY WHY BOTHER GOING OUTSIDE FIRST?
Z

CALVIN, I HOPE YOU TOOK YOUR BOOTS OFF BEFORE YOU WALKED ACROSS THE FLOOR.
OF COURSE I DID! YOU DON'T NEED TO TELL ME ALL THE TIME!
WATTERSON

WATTERSON
GIVEN ANY MORE THOUGHT TO THAT BACKYARD SKI LIFT PROPOSAL OF MINE?
OH, YES. LOTS.

HOBBES IS ALWAYS A LITTLE LOOPY WHEN HE COMES OUT OF THE DRYER.
WATTERSON

Calvin and HOBBES
by WATTERSON
WHAT A DAY!
...AND NO ONE TO SHARE IT WITH!
WOO HOO HOO, IT'S COLD OUT THERE TODAY!
BRRRR! BRISK! JUST THE WAY I LIKE IT! WOW!
SNIFF HA! WEATHER LIKE THIS LETS YOU KNOW YOU'RE ALIVE!
C'MON OUT, GANG! IT'S A PERFECT DAY! YOU'LL GET USED TO THE WIND IF YOU KEEP MOVING!
HEY, C'MON! ARE YOU GUYS JUST GOING TO STAY INSIDE ALL DAY?!?
SHUT THE DUMB DOOR!!
OK, OK! I WAS ON MY WAY BACK OUTSIDE ANYWAY! ...SHEESH...
THERE'S ONE IN EVERY HOUSE.
JUST HOW LONG DID YOU KNOW DAD BEFORE YOU MARRIED HIM?
WATTERSON

WHATCHA DOIN'?
I'M WRITING MY AUTOBIOGRAPHY.
BUT YOU'RE JUST SIX YEARS OLD.
I'VE ONLY GOT ONE SHEET OF PAPER.
WATTERSON

HI, HOBBES. ARE YOU READING THAT BOOK I GAVE YOU?
YES. IT'S VERY GOOD.
YOU LIKE IT?
SURE. I THINK IT'S...
WAIT A MINUTE.
WOULD YOU MIND WRITING IT IN TWO PAGES FOR ME BY TOMORROW MORNING?
WATTERSON

MOM, WAS I ADOPTED?
NO, WHY DO YOU ASK?
ARE YOU PLANNING TO PUT ME TO WORK IN A CANNERY FOR 14 HOURS A DAY WHEN I TURN SEVEN?
OF COURSE NOT!
YOU'RE NOT JUST FATTENING ME UP TO EAT ME, ARE YOU?
GOOD HEAVENS, CALVIN! WHO PUT ALL THESE RIDICULOUS IDEAS IN YOUR HEAD?!?
THAT'S RIGHT. "RIDICULOUS IDEAS" SHE CALLED THEM.
OH, SURE, YOU THINK YOUR MOM'S GOING TO TELL YOU?
WATTERSON

WHIFFFFF
WHIFF
WHIFF
WHIFF
WHIFF
WHIFF
FOR ALL THAT PREPARATION, YOU SURE ARE A LOUSY SHOT!
WATTERSON

GO AHEAD DOWN. YOU'LL MISS ALL THOSE TREES.
YOU CAN DO IT. YOU'LL STOP BEFORE YOU GO OVER THAT LEDGE AT THE BOTTOM.
YOU WON'T GO INTO THAT POND. BESIDES, THE ICE IS PROBABLY REAL THICK ANYWAY. GO AHEAD DOWN.
MY BRAIN IS TRYING TO KILL ME.
WATTERSON

GALOSH
GALOSH
GALOSH
WATTERSON

Calvin and HOBBES
by WATTERSON
BOY, IS THIS HILL BIG! WE'LL HAVE A GOOD LONG RIDE DOWN!
PROVIDED WE IMPROVE OUR STEERING.
HOBBES, DO YOU THINK HUMAN NATURE IS GOOD OR EVIL?
WATCH OUT FOR THOSE TREES.
I MEAN, DO YOU THINK PEOPLE ARE BASICALLY GOOD, WITH A FEW BAD TENDENCIES, OR BASICALLY BAD, WITH A FEW GOOD TENDENCIES?
THERE'S A ROCK UP AHEAD! LOOK OUT!
OR, AS A THIRD POSSIBILITY, DO YOU THINK PEOPLE ARE JUST CRAZY, AND WHO KNOWS WHY THEY DO ANYTHING?
NOT SO CLOSE TO THE LEDGE!
WELL? WHAT DO YOU THINK? ARE PEOPLE GOOD, BAD OR CRAZY?
AUGHHH! I CAN'T LOOK!
WUMP!
YOU KNOW, IT'S VERY RUDE OF YOU TO KEEP CHANGING THE SUBJECT AFTER EVERY SENTENCE.
I CHOOSE CRAZY.
WATTERSON

I CALLED SUSIE A BOOGER-BRAIN AFTER SCHOOL, AND SHE WENT HOME CRYING.
GOODNESS, WHY'D YOU DO **THAT**?
I DUNNO. I WAS JUST TEASING.
IT SOUNDS LIKE YOU HURT HER FEELINGS.
I DIDN'T MEAN FOR HER TO TAKE THE INSULT **PERSONALLY**!
WATERSON

SNIFF THAT STUPID CALVIN. WHY DOES HE CALL ME NAMES FOR NO REASON? IT'S JUST MEAN.
I WISH I HAD A HUNDRED FRIENDS. **THEN** I WOULDN'T CARE. I'D SAY, "WHO NEEDS **YOU**, CALVIN? I'VE GOT A HUNDRED OTHER FRIENDS!"
THEN MY HUNDRED FRIENDS AND I WOULD GO DO SOMETHING FUN, AND LEAVE CALVIN ALL ALONE! HA!
...AND AS LONG AS I'M DREAMING, I'D LIKE A PONY.
WATERSON

I FEEL BAD THAT I CALLED SUSIE NAMES AND HURT HER FEELINGS.
I'M SORRY I DID IT.
MAYBE YOU SHOULD APOLOGIZE TO HER.
I KEEP HOPING THERE'S A LESS OBVIOUS SOLUTION.
WATERSON

"STICKS AND STONES MAY BREAK MY BONES, BUT WORDS WILL NEVER HURT ME."
YEAH, RIGHT.
WATTERSON

UM... HI, SUSIE.. I... UH... WELL...
GET LOST, CALVIN. YOU'RE MEAN.
DON'T WALK AWAY! I'M TRYING TO APOLOGIZE, YOU DUMB NOODLELOAF!
SLAP
WATTERSON

SUSIE, I'M SORRY I CALLED YOU NAMES. I DIDN'T MEAN TO HURT YOUR FEELINGS.
WELL, YOU DID HURT MY FEELINGS, BUT I ACCEPT YOUR APOLOGY. THANK YOU.
WATTERSON
OH BOY, THANK GOODNESS I GOT THAT OVER WITH!
...ON SECOND THOUGHT, LET'S SEE YOU GROVEL A LITTLE BIT!

Calvin and HOBBES
by WATTERSON
SHOULD I OR SHOULDN'T I?
TOO LATE! I DID.
WAP!
DID YOU THROW A SNOWBALL AT ME?!
ME? A SNOWBALL? DID SOMEONE THROW A SNOWBALL AT YOU?
OH, DON'T PLAY INNOCENT WITH ME, YOU LIAR! I KNOW YOU THREW THAT!
CALL ME A LIAR, WILL YOU? WELL, IT TAKES ONE TO KNOW ONE, MR. TAPIOCA HEAD!
OOH! AN INSULT! I'VE BEEN MALIGNED! I'LL NEVER SPEAK TO YOU AGAIN!
HMPH. PROMISES, PROMISES!
OH YEAH? THBBTH BPTHH!
YEAH! THBTH BBPTB!
THBPP THBBTH! BPTH!
THIS IS YOU: AGGLE AGGLE AGGLE!
THIS IS YOU: AA-AAUUAUU-AUAA!
OH YEAH? THIS IS YOU: GAKKA WAKKA WAKKA!
WELL, YOU GO LIKE THIS: DUHH DAHH DAHH DUHH!
CALVIN, TIME TO COME IN!
LEAVE IT TO MOM TO INTERRUPT OUR REPARTEE.
...JUST WHEN I HAD YOU WRIGGLING IN THE CRUSHING GRIP OF REASON TOO...
WATTERSON

HEY, HOBBES, YOU GOT A LETTER.
A LETTER? FOR ME? WOW. I NEVER GET LETTERS!
WATTERSON
WHAT FUN! A LETTER FOR ME! I WONDER WHO SENT IT? I WONDER WHAT IT SAYS? WHAT COULD THIS POSSIBLY BE?
OPEN IT AND FIND OUT, YOU LUNATIC!
DON'T GET HUFFY. I WANT TO SAVOR THIS.

WELL? WELL? WHAT'D YOU GET?
IT LOOKS LIKE AN INVITATION.
AN INVITATION? WHO'D INVITE YOU ANYWHERE?
A LOT OF PEOPLE, THAT'S WHO, BUSTER.
THERE'S OBVIOUSLY BEEN SOME MISTAKE. NOBODY INVITES A TIGER ANYWHERE. YOU CAN'T GET THE INSURANCE.
WELL SOMEBODY IS INVITING ME SOMEWHERE. I GOT AN INVITATION.
WATTERSON
WHO? WHAT'S IT SAY?? READ IT ALREADY!!
PROBABLY SOME BIG STATE DINNER. I HOPE I CAN FIND MY CUMMERBUND.

SO WHAT DOES THE INVITATION SAY, YOU DUMB HAIRBALL?
CALL ME NAMES, WILL YOU? I'LL READ IT WHEN I'M GOOD AND READY.
AARGGHH! OOOOHH! MPF! GGH! RRGGHGHMFMPF!
OK, NOW I'M READY... AHEM..
WATTERSON
"DEAR"
"HOBBES"
FASTER!

WELL, WELL! IT'S AN INVITATION TO SUSIE DERKINS' BIRTHDAY PARTY. HOW NICE.
SUSIE INVITED YOU? WHAT ABOUT ME? DOES IT SAY ME TOO?
NO, IT DOESN'T SAY ANYTHING ABOUT YOU.
SHE MUST HAVE MAILED MY INVITATION SEPARATELY. SHE PROBABLY WANTED TO INSURE IT SO SHE'LL KNOW IT DIDN'T GET LOST. SOMETIMES THOSE TAKE LONGER.
I'LL HAVE TO SIGN FOR IT AND ALL. I'M SURE SHE'S TAKING NO CHANCES WITH MINE.
OH WAIT. ON THE BACK IT SAYS, "YOU CAN BRING THAT STUPID KID YOU HANG AROUND WITH, IF YOU MUST."

WE GET TO GO TO A BIRTHDAY PARTY!
THAT STUPID SUSIE.
BALLOONS, CAKE, PRESENTS... OH BOY!
SHE WON'T BE GETTING A VERY BIG PRESENT FROM ME, THAT'S FOR SURE.
I BET WE'LL PLAY GAMES, TOO! IT WILL BE FUN!
HMPH.
MAYBE WE'LL PLAY "SPIN THE BOTTLE"!
OH GET REAL!

I'LL MAKE A LIST OF POSSIBLE GIFTS FOR SUSIE'S BIRTHDAY. WHAT SHOULD WE GIVE HER?
HOW ABOUT A MOUTH FULL OF BROKEN TEETH? THAT'S WHAT I'D LIKE TO GIVE HER.
OH, DON'T BE SO CRANKY.
I THINK WE SHOULD GET HER A CAN OF TUNA FISH.
TUNA FISH? WHY WOULD SHE WANT THAT?
WELL, MAYBE SHE WOULDN'T, AND WE COULD OFFER TO TAKE IT BACK..... AND BORROW SOME BREAD, A LITTLE MAYO ...
RIGHT, HOBBES.

SUSIE'S HOUSE IS THE NEXT ONE UP.
THIS IS OUR LAST CHANCE TO NOT SHOW UP AND HAVE A NEW BIKE HORN.

HI, SUSIE. HAPPY BIRTHDAY!
HELLO, CALVIN. THANKS FOR COMING.
OH, LOOK AT YOUR STUFFED TIGER! HE'S WEARING A TIE!
HE'S JUST ADORABLE!
OK, YOU WERE RIGHT. GIRLS FLIP FOR TIES. YOU CAN STOP WINKING AT ME.
C'MON IN.

OK, EVERYONE, THE IDEA OF A SCAVENGER HUNT IS TO BRING BACK AS MANY OF THESE ITEMS AS YOU CAN IN HALF AN HOUR. LET'S GO!
QUICK, HOBBES, WHAT'S THE FIRST ITEM?
AN OLD LICENSE PLATE.
GREAT! I SAW ONE ON THE WAY OVER! C'MON!
GOOD THING I ALWAYS CARRY A SWISS ARMY KNIFE. NOBODY'S COMING, RIGHT?
IS THIS GAME LEGAL?

HERE'S A PAPER PLATE FOR THE BIRTHDAY CAKE, CALVIN.
THANK YOU.
I HOPE IT'S GOOD. I HATE IT WHEN THE BIRTHDAY KID CHOOSES SOMETHING GROSS LIKE COCONUT.
YOU DON'T HAVE TO WORRY. IT'S CHOCOLATE.
OH, GOOD. DID YOU SEE IT?
WATTERSON
HEY! WHO CUT A PIECE OF MY CAKE ALREADY?! I DIDN'T EVEN GET TO BLOW OUT THE CANDLES!!
IT'S NICE AND MOIST, TOO.

GLAD YOU BOTH COULD COME. THANK YOU FOR THE NICE PRESENT. GOOD-BYE.
MOM MAY NOT WANT THIS PIECE OF CAKE AND ICE CREAM WE'RE BRINGING HER.
WATTERSON

HEY! IT SNOWED LAST NIGHT!
OH, BOY! LOOK AT IT ALL! THEY'LL HAVE TO CLOSE THE SCHOOLS!
SNOW EVERYWHERE! IT MUST BE WAIST DEEP!
UNFORTUNATELY, THAT'S A RELATIVE MEASURE.
WATTERSON

Calvin and HOBBES
by WATTERSON
HA HA! YOUR CLEVER LITTLE STRATEGY HAS TRAGICALLY BACKFIRED! LOOK AT THIS JUMP! WATCH AND WEEP, FUZZ FACE!
THAT'S YOUR MOVE, RIGHT? I GET TO GO NOW, RIGHT? IT'S TOO LATE FOR YOU TO CHANGE YOUR MIND, RIGHT?
NOT SO FAST... MY HAND'S STILL ON IT.
JUMP, JUMP, JUMP! I WIN!
YOU WIN?!? AAUGGHH! YOU WON LAST TIME! I HATE IT WHEN YOU WIN!
AARRGGH! MFF! GNNK! I HATE THIS GAME! I HATE THE WHOLE WORLD!!
AGHHH! WHAT A STUPID GAME!
YOU MUST HAVE CHEATED! YOU MUST HAVE USED SOME SNEAKY, UNDERHANDED MIND-MELD TO MAKE ME LOSE! I HATE YOU!
I DIDN'T WANT TO PLAY THIS IDIOTIC GAME IN THE FIRST PLACE!
I KNEW YOU'D CHEAT! I KNEW YOU'D WIN!
OH! OOH! AARG!
AAAAAAAAAAAAAAA
AHHAAAAAA AAAAAAHHH...
HACK
PANT
PANT
WATERSON
LOOK, IT'S JUST A GAME.
I KNOW. YOU SHOULD SEE ME WHEN I LOSE IN REAL LIFE!

WHAT'S THE TEACHER HANDING OUT?
OUR REPORT CARDS.
OUR REPORT CARDS?
YOU KNOW, OUR GRADES.
GRADES? WE'RE BEING GRADED?
OF COURSE, DUMMY. WHAT DID YOU THINK?
WATTERSON
DON'T WE EVEN GET A FEW PRACTICE SEMESTERS?

I BROUGHT MY REPORT CARD HOME, DAD.
WELL! LET'S SEE IT!
REMEMBER HOW YOU ONCE TOLD ME IT DIDN'T MATTER WHAT GRADES I GOT...
... JUST SO LONG AS I TRIED MY HARDEST. RIGHT?
WATTERSON
WELL YOU COULD CERTAINLY BE TRYING HARDER THAN THIS!
SO YOU ADMIT YOU WERE LYING?

DAD SAYS MY REPORT CARD SHOWS THAT NOT ENOUGH TIME IS BEING SPENT ON MY HOMEWORK.
SO FROM DINNER TILL BED IS NOW DESIGNATED AS "HOMEWORK TIME."
WATTERSON
I DON'T THINK THAT'S FAIR!
IF IT DOESN'T TAKE THAT LONG TO DO, WHY SHOULD I HAVE TO STAY IN MY ROOM ALL THAT TIME?
YEAH. CAN I HELP IT I'M SO FAST?

CAN I HAVE SOME CLAY?
HELP YOURSELF. THIS STUFF'S IMPOSSIBLE TO WORK WITH.
THANKS.
I'VE GOT A PRETTY GOOD BOWL OR SOMETHING GOING HERE.
IT STARTED OUT AS A PHANTOM JET, BUT IT SORT OF SQUASHED, SO NOW I THINK IT'S A BOWL.
MMM. THAT'S VERY GOOD.
YEAH, I'M REAL PLEASED WITH IT.
WATTERSON

UH OH. THERE'S A DINOSAUR IN THE KITCHEN.
YAARRGH
WELL IF YOU SEE CALVIN ANYWHERE, TELL HIM IT'S ALMOST TIME FOR DINNER.
WATTERSON
I'D INVITE YOU, BUT NO DINOSAURS ARE ALLOWED AT THE DINNER TABLE.
HA. DINOSAURS EAT ANYWHERE THEY WANT.

LET'S GO, CALVIN. TIME FOR YOUR BATH.
I'M NOT TAKING BATHS ANYMORE. I HATE THEM.
OH? AND HOW ARE YOU GOING TO STAY CLEAN?
EASY.
WATTERSON

Calvin and HobbES
by WATTERSON
EITHER HE'S PLAYING CLASSICAL MUSIC AT 78 RPM, OR I'M STILL DREAMING.
FIRST THING TOMORROW MORNING, I'M CALLING THE ORPHANAGE.
WATTERSON

Calvin and HOBBES
by WATTERSON
WHY CAN'T I EVER FIND MY STUPID SCARF?
HOBBES AND I ARE GOING OUTSIDE, MOM.
THIS IS GOING TO BE THE BIGGEST SNOWMAN EVER BUILT!
PEOPLE WILL COME FROM MILES TO SEE OUR GIGANTIC SNOWMAN!
THIS WON'T GO ANY MORE. IT'S TOO BIG TO PUSH.
OK, LEAVE IT HERE.
I'M EXHAUSTED!
WELL WE CAN'T STOP NOW! WE NEED NINE MORE OF THESE!
NINE MORE?!
SURE! THIS IS JUST ONE OF HIS TOES!
WATTERSON

WHERE'S DAD?
HE'S IN THE LIVING ROOM, MAKING A FIRE.
A FIRE! OH, BOY!
OH. IN THE FIREPLACE.
WATTERSON

PIFF!
WANNA CALL THAT A SINGLE, OR GIVE THIS UP?
WATTERSON

WATTERSON
WHAT DID CALVIN WANT WITH THOSE CHRISTMAS LIGHTS?
HE DIDN'T SAY.
UFOS! LAND HERE!
IN THAT CASE, WE'D BETTER CHECK.

WHERE DO WE KEEP ALL OUR CHAINSAWS, MOM?
WATTERSON
WE DON'T HAVE ANY CHAINSAWS, CALVIN.
WE DON'T? NOT ANY?
NOPE.
HOW AM I EVER GOING TO LEARN HOW TO JUGGLE?

THE GIANT AMOEBA SLIDES ALONG THE KITCHEN FLOOR.
EXTENDING A CYTOPLASMIC PSEUDOPOD, THE PROTOZOAN ENGULFS A PACKAGE OF OATMEAL COOKIES.
CRUNCH CRUNCH
NICE TRY. PUT THEM BACK.
WATTERSON

THE MAJESTIC EAGLE CIRCLES SLOWLY IN THE CLOUDS.
WITH EYES SO SHARP HE CAN SPOT MOVEMENT A MILE BELOW, HE SIGHTS HIS PREY AND DIVES!
REACHING SPEEDS OF MORE THAN 100 MPH, HIS UNWARY PRIZE WILL NEVER KNOW WHAT HIT IT!
WATTERSON
WAKE UP, DAD! IT'S SATURDAY!
ZZ... WHA?

Calvin and HOBBES
by WATTERSON
HERE IS SUCCESSFUL MR. JONES. HE LIVES IN A 5-ACRE HOME IN A WEALTHY SUBURB. HERE IS HIS NEW MERCEDES IN THE DRIVEWAY.
IT'S ANYONE'S GUESS AS TO HOW MUCH LONGER MR. JONES CAN MEET HIS MONTHLY FINANCE CHARGES.
HERE COMES MR. JONES OUT OF HIS ATTRACTIVE SUBURBAN HOME. HE HOPS IN HIS RED SPORTS CAR.
OFF HE GOES TO WORK. 80... 90... 100 MILES AN HOUR!
... ALONG THE EDGE OF THE GRAND CANYON !!
SUDDENLY, HIS STEERING LOCKS AND HIS BRAKES FAIL! HE CAREENS OVER THE EDGE! OH NO! DOWN HE GOES!
HIS ONLY HOPE IS TO CLIMB OUT THE SUN ROOF AND JUMP! MAYBE, JUST MAYBE, HE CAN GRAB A BRANCH AND SAVE HIMSELF! HE UNWINDS THE SUN ROOF! CAN HE MAKE IT ??
NO! THE CAR EXPLODES IN MID-AIR, PROPELLING MILLIONS OF TINY SHARDS INTO THE STRATOSPHERE! KABLOOIE!
THE NEIGHBORS HEAR THE BOOM ECHOING ACROSS THE CANYON. THEY PILE INTO A MINI-VAN TO INVESTIGATE! WHAT WILL HAPPEN TO THEM?
WATTERSON

DAD, DID YOU DO A MATING DANCE WHEN YOU FIRST SAW MOM?
A MATING DANCE?
YEAH. I SAW SOME BIRDS DO IT ON TV.
THEY WENT, "AWK AWK BRAAU-AUUKKK!"
YES, THAT'S MORE OR LESS HOW I REACTED.
TO WHAT, WISE GUY? ...THINK CAREFULLY.
WATTERSON

OUT YOU GO, HOBBES. INTO THE DRYER.
RRRRRR
DING!
GOODNESS, YOU'RE A FRIGHT.
TELL YOUR MOM TO PUT SOME CONDITIONER IN THE WASH NEXT TIME.
WATTERSON

I CLEANED MY ROOM, MOM.
AND I EVEN DID IT WITHOUT YOU TELLING ME TO.
WELL, THAT WAS VERY THOUGHTFUL.
OF COURSE, THIS ISN'T GOING TO BE A HABIT OR ANYTHING!
WATTERSON

HOW COME IT DOESN'T TAKE YOU AS LONG AS MOM TO VACUUM THE HOUSE?
MAYBE I'M MORE EFFICIENT.
MAYBE YOU DON'T DO AS GOOD A JOB.
WHY DON'T YOU GO FIND SOMETHING TO DO, MR. CRITIC?
OK, CAN I TAKE THIS DUST BALL IN FOR "SHOW AND TELL" TOMORROW?
CALVIN, THIS DUST BALL IS GOING TO BE OUR LITTLE SECRET, ALL RIGHT?
AAACCK! LOOK AT THIS THING! DEAR, I THOUGHT YOU DID THIS ROOM!
WATTERSON

I'VE BEEN IN THE WATER ABOUT 20 MINUTES. LOOK AT MY FINGERS.
THEY'RE ALL WRINKLED!
SO ARE MY TOES!
PRETTY NEAT, HUH?
WATTERSON
"BIG PINK RAISIN DISCOVERED IN TUB-- BOY'S WHEREABOUTS UNKNOWN!"
AAUGH!

FOR THE NEXT 60 SECONDS, I WILL CONDUCT A TEST OF MY EMERGENCY BROADCAST EQUIPMENT.
WATTERSON
HAD THIS BEEN A REAL EMERGENCY, THE SCREAM YOU JUST HEARD WOULD HAVE BEEN FOLLOWED BY LOTS MORE JUST LIKE IT. THIS CONCLUDES MY...
OH, SOMEDAY WHEN THE HOUSE CAVES IN, SHE'LL THANK ME. MARK MY WORDS.

Calvin and HOBBES
by WATTERSON
AAAAAHHH! EEEE! HEE HEE HEEHEE! WOO! ACK! HE
I'VE GOT YOU!
AAAHEEEEEEEEE
TICKLE TICKLE!
AH! AH! HEE HEE HEE WOO HOO!
I'M GONNA GETCHA! I'M COMING AFTER YOU!
EEK! HEE HEE
HERE I COME!
EEEEE
EEEEE
GOTCHA! GOOTCHIE GOOTCHIE!
AKPTH! HA HAHA
EEEP! HA HA HEE HEE OOH! OOH! HA HA HA!
TICKLE TICKLE!
WATTERSON
WHOA! WHOA! WE'D BETTER STOP. CALM DOWN, CALM DOWN.
HA HA HOO HOO HEE HEE HA
HEE HEE WHOOF! HA HA! (PANT PANT) HEE HEE HEE WHEEEEEEE..
WHOO!
HER PLAN BACKFIRED, DAD. I'M ALL WOUND UP, AND MOM NEEDS TO BE PUT TO BED.
Z

OH, MOM, I NEED SOME CRISCO FOR SCHOOL TODAY!
CHOCOLATE FROSTED SUGAR BOMBS
NEW!
SHORTENING? HONESTLY, CALVIN, I WISH YOU'D REMEMBER THESE THINGS THE NIGHT BEFORE. NOW HURRY UP AND GET READY.
RIGHT.
HERE'S THE CRISCO BACK. THANKS.
YOU PUT IT IN YOUR HAIR??
GET BACK HERE! YOU'RE NOT GOING TO SCHOOL LIKE THAT!
AW C'MON, MOM! IT'S CLASS PICTURE DAY!
WATTERSON

WHAT'S WITH YOUR HAIR?
I TOLD MOM I'M GETTING MY SCHOOL PICTURE TAKEN TODAY, AND SHE MADE ME COMB OUT THE CRISCO I PUT IN MY HAIR. NOW I LOOK LIKE A MORON.
THAT'S TRUE. YOU DO.
WELL DON'T JUST STAND THERE! THINK OF SOMETHING! WHAT CAN I DO?
THERE. MUCH BETTER!
WHAT'D YOU DO? IS IT COOL? IS IT NEW WAVE? GEE, I WISH I HAD A MIRROR...
WATTERSON

THE BUS IS GOING TO BE HERE ANY MINUTE. YOU'RE SURE YOU FIXED MY HAIR SO IT LOOKS OK?
IT LOOKS GREAT. TRY NOT TO MUSS IT UP.
YOU'RE NOT KIDDING ME, ARE YOU? THIS REALLY LOOKS GOOD?
TRUST ME. YOU LOOK LIKE ... LIKE...
WATTERSON
..."ASTRO BOY."
ALL RIGHT! I CAN'T WAIT TO GET MY PICTURE TAKEN NOW!

CALVIN! WHAT DID YOU DO TO YOUR HAIR?? DON'T YOU KNOW WE HAVE OUR PICTURES TAKEN TODAY?
OF COURSE, SILLY. THAT'S WHY I DID IT. IT'S CRISCO.
DOES YOUR MOM KNOW YOU LOOK LIKE THAT?
SORT OF. HOBBES FIXED ME UP A LITTLE AT THE BUS STOP.
WOW. I WISH *I* HAD SOME CRISCO.
WAIT TILL MOM SENDS MY PICTURE TO GRANDMA!
WATTERSON

OK, KID, SIT UP STRAIGHT ON THE STOOL AND LOOK RIGHT AT ME. THAT'S IT.
ARE YOU READY TO TAKE MY PICTURE? SHOULD I TAKE OFF MY SHIRT NOW?
KID, WHAT ARE...? DON'T TAKE OFF YOUR SHIRT!!
SEE? I PAINTED A FACE ON MY STOMACH.
KID, PUT YOUR SHIRT BACK ON.
BUT LOOK! WHEN I BREATHE OUT, THE FACE CHANGES! SEE? OK, TAKE ONE QUICK!
WATTERSON

LOOK, HOBBES, I GOT MY SCHOOL PICTURES BACK.
WATTERSON
LOOK AT YOU! HA HA HA! LOOK AT YOUR HAIR! HEE HEE! THESE ARE GREAT!
AREN'T THEY, THOUGH?
HEE HEE HEE! LOOK AT THIS ONE! WHAT AN EXPRESSION! HOO HOO HOO! HA HA!
YEAH, SEE HOW I GOT MY ONE EYE TO ROLL BACK?
HA HA HA! YOUR MOTHER'S GOING TO GO INTO CONNIPTIONS, OF COURSE..
OH, C'MON. YEARS FROM NOW, THINK OF THE MEMORIES THESE WILL BRING.

Calvin and HOBBES
by WATTERSON
GLIK
GLIK
GLIK
OH NO! WHAT HAVE I DONE?!?
THE HUMAN BODY IS 80% WATER. LITTLE DID CALVIN REALIZE HOW CRITICAL IT IS TO MAINTAIN THAT!
NOW IT'S TOO LATE! BY DRINKING THAT EXTRA GLASS OF WATER, CALVIN HAS UPSET THAT PRECIOUS BALANCE! HE IS NOW 90% WATER!
EVERYTHING SOLID IN CALVIN'S BODY BEGINS TO DISSOLVE!
HE IS BECOMING A LIQUID!!
HIS ONLY HOPE IS SOMEHOW TO GET TO AN ICEBOX AND FREEZE HIMSELF SOLID UNTIL HE CAN GET PROPER MEDICAL ATTENTION!
UNFORTUNATELY, AS A LIQUID, CALVIN CAN ONLY RUN DOWNHILL! CAN HE MAKE IT? CAN HE MAKE IT??
I DON'T THINK I'M GONNA MAKE IT.
THERE'S A GAS STATION UP AHEAD. JUST HOLD ON.
DIDN'T I TELL YOU NOT TO DRINK SO MUCH BEFORE WE LEFT?!
WATTERSON

CALVIN, HOW DO YOU EXPLAIN THIS TEST SCORE? IT'S TERRIBLE!
I DIDN'T STUDY FOR IT.
WHAT DO YOU MEAN YOU DIDN'T STUDY FOR IT? WHY NOT?
I FORGOT.
YOU FORGOT? HOW COULD YOU POSSIBLY FORGET??
WHAT? HUH? WHERE AM I? WHO AM I?
DON'T GIVE ME THIS AMNESIA STUFF!

GEE, IT WAS AWFULLY NICE OF YOU STRANGERS TO HAVE ME OVER FOR DINNER.
CALVIN, KNOCK IT OFF.
YOU MEAN ME? IS MY NAME CALVIN?
YOU'RE NOT FOOLING ANYONE, YOUNG MAN. YOU DO NOT HAVE AMNESIA.
THIS ALL SEEMS VAGUELY FAMILIAR ... AND YET... ...AND YET...
YOU'RE ASKING FOR AN EARLY BEDTIME, KID.
WELL, HE SEEMS TO REMEMBER HE LIKES DESSERT, ANYWAY.
THIS IS "DESSERT," YOU SAY? HMM... PERHAPS MY MEMORY WOULD RETURN IF I HAD SOME MORE.
THAT'S IT. BED!

I'VE HAD ENOUGH OF THIS SILLY AMNESIA GAME. SINCE YOU WON'T STOP IT, YOU'RE GOING TO BED.
YOU CAN LET ME KNOW IF YOU WANT TO BE SERIOUS.
* WINK *
AAUUGHH! MISTER, THERE'S A TIGER IN THIS ROOM!!

CALVIN, ALL WE WANT IS FOR YOU TO STUDY AND DO YOUR BEST IN SCHOOL. EDUCATION IS VERY IMPORTANT.
THAT'S WHY THIS AMNESIA GAME HAS TO STOP. NO MORE "FORGETTING" TO DO YOUR HOMEWORK.
OK?
OK, MISTER.
OK?
...UH, DAD. RIGHT, DAD. YOU GOT IT.
WATTERSON

I'M GLAD TO SEE YOU'RE DOING YOUR HOMEWORK. HOW IS YOUR MATH CLASS GOING NOW?
UM... I'M DOING GREAT.
HOW GREAT?
WATTERSON
REAL GREAT.
HAVE YOU BEEN PASSING ALL YOUR QUIZZES?
I DIDN'T SAY PHENOMENAL.

RING RING
RING RING
RI---
IT'S NEVER FOR ME AND I HATE TAKING MESSAGES.
WATTERSON

Calvin and HOBBES
by WATTERSON
beep beep
!
WATTERSON
I'M HOME!
WAAAA!
AAUUGH!
I THOUGHT THAT AFTER SEVEN BORING HOURS AT SCHOOL, YOU MIGHT APPRECIATE ONE MOMENT OF PURE, ABJECT TERROR.
LET ME UP TO GET MY BAT AND I'LL THANK YOU.

HOBBES, LOOK! THERE'S A LITTLE RACCOON ON THE GROUND.
IS IT ALIVE?
I THINK SO, BUT HE'S HURT. SEE, HE'S HARDLY BREATHING.
BETTER NOT TOUCH HIM IF HE'S HURT.
YEAH. YOU WAIT HERE AND GUARD HIM. I'LL RUN AND GET MOM.
I SURE HOPE SHE CAN HELP.
OF COURSE SHE CAN! YOU DON'T GET TO BE MOM IF YOU CAN'T FIX EVERYTHING JUST RIGHT.
WATTERSON

THERE'S HOBBES GUARDING HIM, MOM. THE LITTLE RACCOON'S RIGHT OVER THERE!
OOH, CALVIN, I DON'T KNOW IF WE CAN SAVE HIM. HE LOOKS PRETTY BAD. GO GET A SHOE BOX AND A CLEAN DISH TOWEL.
RIGHT!
I DON'T THINK THIS POOR LITTLE GUY IS GOING TO MAKE IT, HOBBES. (SIGH) I HATE IT WHEN THESE THINGS HAPPEN.
...YOU CAN TELL I'M UPSET WHEN I START TALKING TO ***YOU***...
WATTERSON

WELL, I GOT HIM IN THE SHOE BOX. I GUESS ALL WE CAN DO IS KEEP HIM WARM AND SAFE.
WE'LL KEEP HIM IN THE GARAGE, AND PUT OUT SOME WATER AND FOOD.
I READ IN A BOOK THAT RACCOONS WILL EAT JUST ABOUT ANYTHING.
WATTERSON
CHANCES ARE, I'LL BE HAPPY TO DONATE MOST OF MY DINNER.
CALVIN, YOU DON'T EVEN KNOW WHAT WE'RE HAVING.

HAS HE EATEN ANYTHING?
NO.
DON'T DIE, LITTLE RACCOON.
IT WOULDN'T BE VERY GRATEFUL OF YOU TO BREAK MY HEART.
HOONK
WATTERSON

I CAN'T SLEEP.
ME EITHER. I KEEP THINKING ABOUT THE RACCOON.
I HOPE HE LIVES.
ME TOO.
I THINK ANIMALS ARE ALWAYS SO CUTE.
WATTERSON

DAD, DID YOU CHECK ON THE LITTLE RACCOON THIS MORNING?
YES, CALVIN. ...I'M AFRAID HE DIED.
WAAHHHH!!
I'M SORRY TOO, KIDDO. BUT HE DIDN'T HAVE MUCH OF A CHANCE.
WAHH AAHH!
AT LEAST HE DIED WARM AND SAFE, CALVIN. WE DID ALL WE COULD, BUT NOW HE'S GONE.
SNIFF ...I KNOW. I'M CRYING BECAUSE OUT THERE HE'S GONE, BUT HE'S NOT GONE INSIDE ME.
WATTERSON

THIS IS WHERE DAD BURIED THE LITTLE RACCOON.
I DIDN'T EVEN KNOW HE EXISTED A FEW DAYS AGO AND NOW HE'S GONE FOREVER. IT'S LIKE I FOUND HIM FOR NO REASON. I HAD TO SAY GOOD-BYE AS SOON AS I SAID HELLO.
STILL... IN A SAD, AWFUL, TERRIBLE WAY, I'M HAPPY I MET HIM.
SNIFF
WHAT A STUPID WORLD.
WATTERSON

YOU KNOW, HOBBES, I CAN'T FIGURE OUT THIS DEATH STUFF.
WHY DID THAT LITTLE RACCOON HAVE TO DIE? HE DIDN'T DO ANYTHING WRONG.
HE WAS JUST LITTLE! WHAT'S THE POINT OF PUTTING HIM HERE AND TAKING HIM BACK SO SOON?!?
IT'S EITHER MEAN OR IT'S ARBITRARY, AND EITHER WAY I'VE GOT THE HEEBIE-JEEBIES.
WHY IS IT ALWAYS NIGHT WHEN WE TALK ABOUT THESE THINGS?
WATTERSON

MOM SAYS DEATH IS AS NATURAL AS BIRTH, AND IT'S ALL PART OF THE LIFE CYCLE.
SHE SAYS WE DON'T REALLY UNDERSTAND IT, BUT THERE ARE MANY THINGS WE DON'T UNDERSTAND, AND WE JUST HAVE TO DO THE BEST WE CAN WITH THE KNOWLEDGE WE HAVE.
I GUESS THAT MAKES SENSE.
...BUT DON'T *YOU* GO ANYWHERE.
DON'T WORRY.
WATTERSON

Calvin and Hobbes
by WATTERSON
HERE'S A PHOTO I TOOK OF YOU.
THE PICTURE IS KIND OF FUZZY.
YOU'RE KIND OF FUZZY!
OK, MAKE A FACE!
HOWTH THITH?
GREAT! HOLD IT!
POOF
LET'S SEE! LET'S SEE!
IT'S DEVELOPING! I CAN START TO SEE IT!
THERE I AM! LOOK! LOOK!
HA! HA! IT'S GREAT! WHAT A PHOTOGRAPH!
HEE HEE HOO HOO HA HA!
HA HA HEE HEE HO HO HO!
LET'S TAKE SOME MORE! THAT'S IT, BUG YOUR EYES OUT!
HEE HEE! HURRY UP!
WATTERSON
ALL THESE PICTURES ARE OF HOBBES?!
AREN'T THEY A SCREAM? CAN I HAVE TEN BUCKS FOR ANOTHER ROLL OF FILM?

HEY! WHAT HAPPENED TO THE TREES HERE? WHO CLEARED OUT THE WOODS?
THERE USED TO BE LOTS OF ANIMALS IN THESE WOODS! NOW IT'S A MUD PIT!
THIS SIGN SAYS, "FUTURE SITE OF SHADY ACRES CONDOMINIUMS."
ANIMALS CAN'T AFFORD CONDOS!
"SHADY ACRES"? THE ONLY SHADE I SEE IS FROM THAT BULLDOZER.
WATTERSON

WHERE ARE ALL THE ANIMALS SUPPOSED TO LIVE NOW THAT THEY CUT DOWN THESE WOODS TO PUT IN HOUSES??
BY GOLLY, HOW WOULD PEOPLE LIKE IT IF ANIMALS BULLDOZED A SUBURB AND PUT IN NEW TREES?!?
WATTERSON
NO GOOD. THEY DIDN'T LEAVE THE KEYS.

IT TOOK HUNDREDS OF YEARS FOR THESE WOODS TO GROW, AND THEY LEVELED IT IN A WEEK. IT'S GONE.
AFTER THEY BUILD NEW HOUSES HERE, THEY'LL HAVE TO WIDEN THE ROADS AND PUT UP GAS STATIONS, AND PRETTY SOON THIS WHOLE AREA WILL JUST BE A BIG STRIP.
EVENTUALLY THERE WON'T BE A NICE SPOT LEFT ANYWHERE.
I WONDER IF YOU CAN REFUSE TO INHERIT THE WORLD.
I THINK IF YOU'RE BORN, IT'S TOO LATE.
WATTERSON

Calvin and HOBBES
by WATTERSON
KABLOOIE!
OOOOH, YOU'VE TWICKED ME FOR THE WAST TIME, WABBIT!
HA HA HA! BOY, I WISH I HAD SOME DYNAMITE!
BOY, I LOVE WEEKENDS! WHAT BETTER WAY TO SPEND ONE'S FREEDOM THAN EATING CHOCOLATE CEREAL AND WATCHING CARTOONS!
MM... I BEG TO DIFFER ON THE CEREAL PART.
CALVIN, YOU'VE BEEN SITTING IN FRONT OF THAT STUPID TV ALL MORNING! IT'S A BEAUTIFUL DAY! YOU SHOULD BE OUTSIDE!
IT'S GOING TO BE A GRIM DAY WHEN THE WORLD IS RUN BY A GENERATION THAT DOESN'T KNOW ANYTHING BUT WHAT IT'S SEEN ON TV!
click
HEY!
HOW CAN YOU SIT INSIDE ALL DAY? GO ON! OUT! OUT!
KIDS ARE SUPPOSED TO RUN AROUND IN THE FRESH AIR! HAVE SOME FUN! GET SOME EXERCISE!
WATTERSON
SLAM!
WELL, I GUESS THAT'S THAT. COME ON.
HI, SUSIE, ARE YOU WATCHING TV? CAN WE COME IN?
SURE, HURRY UP! IT'S A COMMERCIAL.

HOBBES, WANT TO SEE MY TRANSMOGRIFIER?
I DIDN'T KNOW YOU HAD A TRANSMOGRIFIER.
I JUST GOT IT.
YOU STEP INTO THIS CHAMBER, SET THE APPROPRIATE DIALS, AND IT TURNS YOU INTO WHATEVER YOU'D LIKE TO BE.
TRANSMOG-RIFIER
IT'S AMAZING WHAT THEY DO WITH CORRUGATED CARDBOARD THESE DAYS.
ISN'T IT?
TRANSMOG-RIFIER

THIS TRANSMOGRIFIER WILL TURN YOU INTO ANYTHING AT ALL.
TRANSMOG-RIFIER
ALL YOU DO IS SET THIS INDICATOR, AND THE MACHINE AUTOMATICALLY RESTRUCTURES YOUR CHEMICAL CONFIGURATION. YOU CAN BE AN EEL, A BABOON, A GIANT BUG, OR A DINOSAUR.
Eel
Baboon
Bug
Dino-saur
WHAT IF YOU WANT TO BE SOMETHING ELSE?
I LEFT SOME ROOM. JUST WRITE IT ON THE SIDE.

WELL, WHAT DO YOU SAY? WOULD YOU LIKE TO BE TRANSMOGRIFIED?
TRANSMOG-RIFIER
I DON'T THINK SO. BEING A TIGER IS MY AREA OF EXPERTISE.
DON'T BE SCARED. THE PROCESS IS INSTANTANEOUS AND COMPLETELY PAINLESS.
JUST THINK! WITH THE PUSH OF A BUTTON, YOU COULD BE A 500-STORY GASTROPOD – A SLUG THE SIZE OF THE CHRYSLER BUILDING!
GOSH, HOW CAN I REFUSE?
WELL IF YOU DON'T LIKE THAT, BE SOMETHING ELSE! I DON'T CARE!

LOOK, IF YOU CAN'T MAKE UP YOUR MIND, ***I'LL*** GO FIRST AND TURN MYSELF INTO SOMETHING.
I'LL SHOW YOU.
BUT WHAT'S THE POINT OF TURNING YOURSELF INTO SOMETHING ELSE?
NO ONE'S DONE IT! THINK OF THE KNOWLEDGE TO BE GAINED!
WHAT HORRORS WE VISIT UPON OURSELVES IN THE NAME OF SCIENCE.
OK, I'M IN. SET THE DIAL ON "LUNGFISH." ..NO, MAKE IT "MUSK OX." ...NO ...

WHAT ARE YOU GOING TO TRANSMOGRIFY INTO?
HOW ABOUT A TIGER?
THAT'S A GOOD IDEA. THE WORLD CAN ALWAYS USE ANOTHER TIGER.
JUST TURN THE ARROW AND PUSH THE BUTTON, THEN.
ALL RIGHT, HERE YOU GO.
ZAP!
DID IT WORK?
BOY, I'M HOT. HOW DO YOU STAND HAVING ALL THIS FUR?
TRANSMO RIFIER

SO YOU'RE A TIGER NOW?
YEP. LET ME OUT.
WORDS FAIL ME.
I'M DISAPPOINTED TOO, BUT KEEP IN MIND TRANSMOGRIFICATION IS A NEW TECHNOLOGY.

SO CALVIN, WHAT'S IT LIKE TO BE A TIGER NOW?
KINDA FUZZY, BUT NOT THAT DIFFERENT.
SO! WHAT DO YOU WANT TO TALK ABOUT?
DO WE EAT SOON?

HI, MOM! WILL YOU MAKE HOBBES AND ME A BIG TUNA SANDWICH?
I THOUGHT YOU HATED TUNA FISH.
NOT ANYMORE. I'M A TIGER NOW.
I THOUGHT HOBBES WAS YOUR TIGER.
NOW I'M ONE TOO. I TRANSMOGRIFIED.
OH, I SEE.
MY, SHE'S TAKING THIS WELL. BUT THE STRAIN WILL SURELY CRACK HER SOON.

I'M HOME!
HI, DAD. NOTICE ANYTHING DIFFERENT ABOUT ME?
UH... NEW HAIRCUT?
GEEZ, DID YOU GO **BLIND**?? I'M A **TIGER**!
OH, I THOUGHT YOU MEANT ***BESIDES*** THAT. CALVIN, YOUR DAD'S VERY TIRED, AND...
HOPE YOU WANT TUNA FOR DINNER, DEAR..

WELL, HOBBES, IT'S BEEN FUN, BUT I DON'T THINK I WAS MEANT TO BE A TIGER.
JUST SET THE DIAL TO "CALVIN," AND I'LL TRANSMOGRIFY BACK TO A BOY.
HERE YOU GO.
TRANSMOG-RIFIER
ZAP!
OOPS!
TRY AGAIN, LUNKHEAD.

HERE I AM, BACK TO BEING CALVIN.
YOUR MACHINE WORKS AMAZINGLY WELL.
IT'S MY OWN DESIGN.
WHAT WILL YOU DO WITH IT NOW?
GOOD QUESTION.
...ALTHOUGH I SUPPOSE WE COULD TURN SUSIE INTO A BOWL OF CHOWDER IF WE COULD JUST GET HER IN THE MACHINE.
LEAVE ME OUT OF YOUR LIFE'S PLANS, YOU LITTLE WEIRDO.

CALVIN EATS ONE BITE TOO MANY! HE BEGINS TO SWELL!
INFLATING LIKE A RAFT, HE GROWS BIGGER AND BIGGER!
OH NO! HOW MUCH LARGER CAN HE GET?
OOOOH, I THINK I'M GOING TO EXPLODE.
NO WONDER! I'VE NEVER SEEN ANYONE EAT SO MUCH IN ONE SITTING! I HOPE YOU LEARNED A LITTLE LESSON.

Calvin and HOBBES
by WATTERSON
THANKS FOR THE LUNCH, MOM! I'M GOING OUTSIDE.
REFUELED, THE 727 TAXIS ONTO THE RUNWAY.
CONTROL TOWER TO CALVIN, YOU ARE CLEARED FOR TAKE OFF.
ROGER.
FULL THROTTLE!
FWOOOSHH!
TAKE OFF! LANDING GEAR UP! CHUGUNK!
WE HAVE REACHED OUR CRUISING ALTITUDE OF 30,000 FEET. A SMALL, TASTELESS SNACK WILL BE SERVED SHORTLY.
THIS IS YOUR CAPTAIN SPEAKING. I'M AFRAID OUR ARRIVAL WILL BE SLIGHTLY DELAYED.
WE'RE STACKED UP OVER WASHINGTON, AND WE'LL BE IN A HOLDING PATTERN FOR ANOTHER 40 MINUTES.
TOWER TO CALVIN, YOU ARE NOW CLEARED FOR LANDING.
ROGER. LANDING GEAR DOWN! REVERSE THRUST!
WATTERSON
I SAW YOU OUTSIDE RUNNING IN CIRCLES FOR ALMOST AN HOUR! ARE YOU TRYING TO MAKE YOURSELF SICK?!?
OOG, FROM NOW ON, I'M PLAYING "BUS."

Calvin and HOBBES
by WATTERSON
Look, Jane. See Spot.
See Spot run.
Run, Spot, run.
Jane sees Spot run.
WAY TO GO, JANE!
BOY, I HATE HOMEWORK.
YAHH!
WHOOP!
HEY!
YOW! WHOA! STOP!
GALOOP GALOOP
AAAUGHH!!
GAACKK! HELP! HELP!
WHAP!!
BONK!
BONK!
WHAT ON EARTH ARE YOU DOING? WHERE'S YOUR HOMEWORK?
I COULDN'T CONCENTRATE.

RRINNGGG!
RECESS IS OVER!
R-R-RIPP!
SNAG
OH NO!
WHY IS IT YOU ALWAYS RIP YOUR PANTS ON THE DAY EVERYONE HAS TO DEMONSTRATE A MATH PROBLEM AT THE CHALKBOARD?

I CAN'T BELIEVE I RIPPED MY PANTS! RECESS IS OVER. I'M SUPPOSED TO BE BACK IN CLASS!
I CAN'T GO IN LIKE THIS! WHAT AM I GOING TO DO?!
...OF ALL THE DAYS TO WEAR THE UNDERPANTS WITH THE LITTLE ROCKET SHIPS...

LOOK AT THE SIZE OF THIS RIP! MAYBE I CAN PULL MY SHIRT DOWN OVER IT.
NO, THAT DOESN'T WORK. MAYBE I CAN TUCK MY SHIRT INTO THE HOLE. ..NOPE..
MAYBE I CAN STICK THE RIPPED PART UNDER MY BELT. NO, THAT DOESN'T WORK EITHER.
MAYBE I CAN SCOOT AROUND ON MY REAR THE REST OF THE DAY.

PLEASE DON'T LET THE TEACHER CALL ON ME! DON'T MAKE ME GO TO THE BOARD IN MY RIPPED PANTS!
ANYONE BUT ME! JUST LET HER CALL ON SOMEONE ELSE! PLEASE DON'T EMBARRASS ME IN FRONT OF THE WHOLE CLASS!
CALVIN, WOULD YOU DO THE NEXT PROBLEM AT THE BOARD?
SO MUCH FOR MY EVER JOINING THE CLERGY.
WATTERSON

CALVIN, WILL YOU DO THE NEXT PROBLEM AT THE BOARD, PLEASE?
NO.
WHY NOT?
FRANKLY, I'D RATHER NOT SAY.
OH, YOU WOULDN'T?
IT'S A PERSONAL MATTER.
WATTERSON
YOU'RE GOING TO HAVE TO DO BETTER THAN **THAT**.
DO THE WORDS "COMPLETE PANDEMONIUM" STRIKE TERROR IN YOUR HEART?

SO YOUR TEACHER DIDN'T KNOW YOU'D RIPPED YOUR PANTS, AND SHE MADE YOU DO A PROBLEM AT THE CHALK-BOARD?
THAT SUMS IT UP.
HOW AWFUL! WHAT DID YOU **DO**?!?
I DIDN'T HAVE A CHOICE. I MOONED THE WHOLE CLASS.
THAT'S WHY YOU'RE HOME EARLY?
THREE TEACHERS AND THE PRINCIPAL COULDN'T RESTORE ORDER.
WATTERSON

Calvin and HOBBES
by WATTERSON
"DURING EMERGENCY LANDING, REPLACE DINNER TRAY AND BRING SEAT TO UPRIGHT POSITION. EXTINGUISH ALL SMOKING MATERIALS."
"...INCLUDING SPACECRAFT, IF POSSIBLE."
OUT OF FUEL, THE COURAGEOUS SPACEMAN SPIFF IS FORCED TO LAND ON THE DISTANT PLANET ZOK!
THE VALIANT EXPLORER SURVEYS THE ZOKKIAN LANDSCAPE. WHO KNOWS WHAT DANGERS LIE HIDDEN IN THE CRATERED TERRAIN?
UNDAUNTED, SPIFF SETS OUT TO FIND HELP!
MILES LATER, IT IS EVIDENT THE PLANET IS COMPLETELY UNINHABITED!
OUR HERO IS MAROONED ON A LIFELESS PLANET! ALONE ON AN ALIEN WORLD!
ALONE... ALL ALONE...
!
WATTERSON
DARN IT, WHY DOESN'T ANYONE EVER **TELL** ME WHEN THE LUNCH BELL RINGS?

SUSIE, WHERE'S MISS WORMWOOD? WHO'S THAT LADY AT HER DESK?
MISS WORMWOOD'S SICK. THAT'S OUR SUBSTITUTE TEACHER.
A SUBSTITUTE?
LET'S SEE YOUR TEACHING CERTIFICATE, LADY!

GOOD MORNING, CLASS. I'LL BE YOUR SUBSTITUTE TEACHER TODAY.
MISS WORMWOOD LEFT ME INSTRUCTIONS AS TO WHAT WE NEED TO GO OVER, SO WE SHOULDN'T HAVE ANY PROBLEMS.
OH WAIT, HERE'S A NOTE SHE ADDED. JUST A SECOND...
OK, WHICH ONE OF YOU IS CALVIN?
NOT ME!
WATTERSON

WE HAD A SUBSTITUTE TEACHER IN SCHOOL TODAY.
DID YOU LIKE HER?
SHE WAS OK, I GUESS.
YOU "GUESS"?
IT'S HARD TO SAY.
SHE WENT HOME AT NOON.
WATTERSON

Mr. Jones lives 50 miles away from you. You both leave home at 5:00 and drive toward each other.
Mr. Jones travels at 35 mph., and you drive at 40 mph. At what time will you pass Mr. Jones on the road?
GIVEN THE TRAFFIC AROUND HERE AT 5:00, WHO KNOWS?
I ALWAYS CATCH THESE TRICK QUESTIONS.
WATTERSON

I'VE GOT A SCHEME TO GET US SOME MONEY.
OH BOY.
SEE? I SNEAKED ALL THESE KERNELS OF CORN OFF MY DINNER PLATE TONIGHT.
HOW IS THAT GOING TO GET US MONEY?
EASY. I JUST STICK THEM UNDER MY PILLOW.
WITH ANY LUCK, THE TOOTH FAIRY WON'T KNOW THEY'RE FAKES UNTIL IT'S TOO LATE!
WATTERSON

DAD, HOW DO PEOPLE MAKE BABIES?
MOST PEOPLE JUST GO TO SEARS, BUY THE KIT, AND FOLLOW THE ASSEMBLY INSTRUCTIONS.
I CAME FROM SEARS?!?
NO, YOU WERE A BLUE LIGHT SPECIAL AT K MART. ALMOST AS GOOD, AND A LOT CHEAPER.
AAUUGHHH!
DEAR, WHAT ARE YOU TELLING CALVIN NOW?!
WATTERSON

Calvin and HOBBES
by WATTERSON
HOW COME YOU DON'T PUT ON ANY PAJAMAS?
FACT IS, I NEVER TAKE 'EM OFF!
DID YOU WASH YOUR FACE AND BRUSH YOUR TEETH?
YEP! WE BOTH DID!
OK THEN, GOOD NIGHT.
GOOD NIGHT.
MOVE OVER, WILL YA?
I'M ALREADY OVER! YOU SHOULD BE OVER THERE!
QUIT PUSHING, FUZZ-FOR-BRAINS! YOU'RE ON MY SIDE!
CALL ME NAMES, WILL YOU?!
YEAH!
WHUMPP!
OH NO!
OK! OK! YOU WIN!
PHOO... I WISH YOU HAD BRUSHED YOUR TEETH!
YECCH... I WISH YOU HAD WASHED YOUR FACE!
WATTERSON

I'VE GOT TO GIVE A 5-MINUTE ORAL REPORT IN SCHOOL ON THURSDAY.
WE'RE SUPPOSED TO RESEARCH OUR SUBJECT, WRITE IT UP, AND PRESENT IT TO THE CLASS WITH A VISUAL AID.
THAT'S A BIG ASSIGNMENT.
I'LL SAY. I HATE MY TEACHER.
SHE KNOWS WE'LL ALL DO IT ON THE LAST EVENING, BUT SHE GAVE US THREE DAYS TO WORRY ABOUT IT.
WATERSON

WHAT'S THE SUBJECT OF YOUR REPORT?
THE BRAIN.
WHAT DO YOU KNOW ABOUT BRAINS?
WELL, I SAW THIS MOVIE WHERE THEY KEPT THIS GUY'S BRAIN ALIVE IN A TANK OF WATER.
THEN A POWER SURGE MUTATED THE BRAIN, AND IT CRAWLED OUT AND TERRORIZED THE POPULACE.
THAT'S INFORMATIVE.
UNFORTUNATELY FOR MY REPORT, MOM CAUGHT ME, AND I DIDN'T GET TO SEE HOW IT ENDED.
WATTERSON

I'VE GOT TO GIVE MY REPORT ON "THE BRAIN" AT SCHOOL TODAY.
SEE MY VISUAL AID? I COOKED SOME NOODLES AND PUT THEM IN A PAPER BAG. DOESN'T THAT LOOK LIKE BRAINS?
UGH.
WATERSON
WELL, I GUESS I'M ALL SET.
DID YOU WRITE YOUR REPORT YET?
NAH. I BORROWED MOM'S POCKET DICTIONARY. I'LL DO IT ON THE BUS.

MY FIVE-MINUTE REPORT IS ON "THE BRAIN."
OF COURSE, IT'S DIFFICULT TO EXPLAIN THE COMPLEXITIES OF THE BRAIN IN JUST FIVE MINUTES, BUT TO BEGIN, THE BRAIN IS PART OF THE CENTRAL NERVOUS SYSTEM.
I'LL PAUSE FOR A FEW MOMENTS, SO YOU ALL CAN FINISH WRITING THAT DOWN.
CALVIN!
WATTERSON

POW! JAB! KICK! POW! POW!
RATTATATTATTATTA RATTATATTATTA
EEEEEEEEEEE
BOOM!
PLEASE, PLEASE, PRETTY PLEASE?
NO. YOU SHOULD'VE SAVED SOME OF YOUR OWN HALLOWEEN CANDY.
WATTERSON

HEY, CAN WE CHANGE THE CHANNEL NOW? I WANT TO WATCH SOMETHING ELSE.
MY SHOW'S NOT OVER YET.
AW C'MON! YOU SEE THIS PROGRAM ALL THE TIME! CAN'T WE WATCH MY SHOW FOR ONCE?
NO, I WAS HERE FIRST. PIPE DOWN. THIS IS A GOOD PART.
AARRGHH
I HATE NATIONAL GEOGRAPHIC ANIMAL SPECIALS.
WATTERSON

Calvin and HOBBES
by WATTERSON
GOOD NIGHT, CALVIN.
...ALL RIGHT, WHERE ARE YOU?!
CALVIN, I THOUGHT I SAID TO GET READY FOR BED! NOW HURRY UP!
I
CAN'T!
I'M
TRAPPED
IN
SLOW
MOTION!
WELL YOU'D BETTER GET IN NORMAL SPEED......
...NOW!
...AHH! TIME SNAP!

Point A is twice as far from point C as point B is from A. If the distance from point B to point C is 5 inches, how far is point A from point C?
THE LIVING DEAD DON'T **NEED** TO SOLVE WORD PROBLEMS.

CALVIN THE ZOMBIE SEARCHES FOR FOOD.
HORRIBLY, THE UNDEAD FEED UPON THE LIVING!
...ALTHOUGH, IN A PINCH, A PBJ WILL DO, IF YOU EAT IT MESSILY ENOUGH.

!
"WHEN IN ROME..."

THPKK! HEE HEE..
GKPTHH! HEH HEH...
!
HEE HEE HOO HOO HA HA HA HA HA HA HA HO HO HEE HEE HO
HEH HEH... OF COURSE, **REAL** ZOMBIES **NEVER** GET THE GIGGLES BY LOOKING AT EACH OTHER.
HEE HEE
WATTERSON

OH NO! TOO MUCH BUBBLE BATH!
UH OH!
WATTERSON
POP!
HOW ON EARTH DO YOU **DO** THIS??!
THESE THINGS JUST SEEM TO HAPPEN.

AAUGHHHH
WATTERSON

Calvin and HOBBES
by WATTERSON
GOSH, IT'S PERFECT KITE FLYING WEATHER!
BUT WHY LET THE STUPID KITE HAVE ALL THE FUN?
YOU'VE GOT YOUR TAIL ON?
YEP. JUST LET OUT SOME STRING AND START RUNNING.
THAT'S IT! FASTER! FASTER!
I'M FLYING! I'M FL-OOF! OW! ACK! OOH!
ARE YOU OK? BOY, YOU WERE ALMOST UP THERE.
I KNOW! (OW.) WE JUST NEED A LITTLE MORE WIND.
OK, HERE'S ANOTHER BREEZE! LET 'ER RIP!
OOMPH! YOW!
AARGHH!
MAYBE YOU'RE TOO HEAVY.
GEE, I HADN'T THOUGHT OF THAT. HMM... HOW CAN I GET LIGHTER?
MRS. CARROLL SAYS A NAKED KID TIED TO A STUFFED ANIMAL IS RUNNING THROUGH HER YARD.
YOU HANDLE IT. I GOT THE LITTLE NUDIST OUT OF HER BIRD BATH, REMEMBER?
WATTERSON

WE'RE SUPPOSED TO HAVE THIS WHOLE STUPID BOOK READ BY TOMORROW.
FLIP-IP-IP-IP-IP-IP!
THERE! IT'S GOOD TO GET **THAT** OUT OF THE WAY!
READING GOES FASTER IF YOU DON'T SWEAT COMPREHENSION.
WHERE'S THE FRISBEE?
WATTERSON

AHOY! TOSS THE ROPE LADDER DOWN!
WHAT'S THE PASSWORD?
"TIGERS ARE MEAN! TIGERS ARE FIERCE! TIGERS HAVE TEETH AND CLAWS THAT PIERCE!"
"TIGERS ARE GREAT! THEY CAN'T BE BEAT! IF I WAS A TIGER, THAT WOULD BE NEAT!"
WATTERSON
HE CAN CLIMB THE TREE WITHOUT THE LADDER, SO **HE** GOT TO MAKE UP THE PASSWORD.
GO ON, WHAT'S THE **THIRD** VERSE?

MOM, WHEN ARE YOU GOING SHOPPING NEXT?
I DON'T KNOW. WHY?
WE SEEM TO BE OUT OF GUN POWDER.
WATTERSON
SHEESH, I DIDN'T EVEN **DO** IT YET.

NOW!
ARE YOU SURE THERE'S A CAREER TO BE MADE AS A "HUMAN DISCUS"?
WELL, WE GOTTA GET A BIGGER FIELD....

I TRIPPED A KID YESTERDAY, AND HE FELL IN THE MUD. IT WAS HILARIOUS.
AAUGH!
TRIP
PLOOP!
I DUNNO. THAT KIND OF HUMOR IS SO BROAD.
YOU DIDN'T DO IT RIGHT. C'MERE AND GIVE ME A HAND.

WHAT'S THIS? IT LOOKS GROSS.
IT'S A VEGETARIAN MEAL. IT'S GOOD FOR YOU.
VEGETARIAN?? YECCHH! I'M NOT A VEGETARIAN!
I'M A DESSERTARIAN.

Calvin and Hobbes
by WATTERSON
EVER NOTICE HOW DIFFERENT THE AIR SMELLS AFTER A GOOD RAIN? IT SMELLS LIKE... LIKE..
DEAD WORMS!
WOW! LOOK AT THE SIZE OF THAT PUDDLE!
WAHOOOOO
HA HA HA HA HA HA
SPLOOSH SPLASH SPLOOSH SPLASH
HEE HEE HEE HEE HA HA HA HA
RATS. MY UNDERWEAR'S ALL SOAKED. NOW IT'S GONNA ITCH AND RIDE UP MY REAR ALL AFTERNOON.
..WELL, IT WAS WORTH IT!
THAT'S WHY I NEVER WEAR THE STUFF.
WATTERSON

I CAN'T GET THIS STUPID HAIR TO COMB RIGHT.
SEE HOW IT STICKS OUT IN BACK?
MAYBE YOU NEED A HAIRCUT.
YEAH, BUT BARBERS NEVER CUT IT THE WAY I WANT.
BOY, WHAT A GREAT IDEA! THANKS!
THIS IS EASY! YOU REALLY THINK YOUR MOM WILL PAY ME EIGHT BUCKS?
WATTERSON

SO EXACTLY HOW WOULD YOU LIKE THE BACK CUT?
JUST TRIM THE PART THAT STICKS OUT AND TAPER IT A LITTLE.
WOULDN'T YOU RATHER HAVE IT REAL SHORT?
NO, JUST CUT A LITTLE BIT.
ARE YOU SURE? DON'T YOU THINK IT SHOULD BE REAL SHORT? IT LOOKS LIKE IT SHOULD BE REAL SHORT.
ARE YOU TRYING TO TELL ME SOMETHING?
NO, I JUST THINK IT SHOULD BE REAL SHORT. ESPECIALLY, OH, RIGHT HERE.
WATTERSON

YOU MADE A MISTAKE, DIDN'T YOU?
NO. I CAN COVER IT UP.
COVER WHAT UP? WHAT DID YOU DO WRONG?
NOTHING. I CAN'T HELP IT IF YOUR HEAD HAS FUNNY BUMPS THAT MAKE THE SCISSORS GO SCREWY.
OOPS. HOLD STILL.
YOUR HEAD'S GONNA HAVE "FUNNY BUMPS" IN A MINUTE IF YOU DON'T TELL ME WHAT YOU DID!!
WHY'D YOU SAY "OOPS"?! WHAT'D YOU DO NOW?!
NOTHING. LET'S TRY PARTING YOUR HAIR FROM EAR TO EAR.
WATTERSON

THIS HAIRCUT HAD BETTER LOOK GOOD, FUZZ BRAIN.
YOU'LL LOVE IT. IT'S KIND OF "NEW WAVE".
NEW WAVE? LIKE HOW?
WELL, SORT OF "PUNK," ACTUALLY.
LIKE A MOHAWK?
IN SOME PLACES IT'S SORT OF LIKE A MOHAWK.
I WANT A MIRROR.
YOU KNOW WHAT'S THE RAGE THIS YEAR? ...HATS.
WATTERSON

LOOK WHAT YOU DID TO MY HAIR! IT LOOKS LIKE IT WAS CUT WITH A WEED-EATER!
NOTHING A LITTLE TONIC AND COMBING CAN'T FIX.
GET AWAY FROM ME, YOU MENACE!
IF MOM SEES THIS, SHE'LL BLOW HER BLOOD VESSELS! WHAT AM I GOING TO DO??
WATTERSON
HOW'S THAT? SORT OF THE "LAWRENCE OF ARABIA" LOOK!
SORT OF THE "LOBOTOMY PATIENT" LOOK.

MY CIGARETTE SMOKE MIXED WITH THE SMOKE OF MY .38. IF BUSINESS WAS AS GOOD AS MY AIM, I'D BE ON EASY STREET. INSTEAD, I'VE GOT AN OFFICE ON 49TH STREET AND A NASTY RELATIONSHIP WITH A STRING OF COLLECTION AGENTS.
YEAH, THAT'S ME, TRACER BULLET. I'VE GOT EIGHT SLUGS IN ME. ONE'S LEAD, AND THE REST ARE BOURBON. THE DRINK PACKS A WALLOP, AND I PACK A REVOLVER. I'M A PRIVATE EYE.
TRACER BULLET
SUDDENLY MY DOOR SWUNG OPEN, AND IN WALKED TROUBLE. BRUNETTE, AS USUAL.
TAKE YOUR HAT OFF AT THE DINNER TABLE, CALVIN. IT'S NOT POLITE.
SHE WAS A PUSHY DAME, BUT SHE HAD A CASE..
WATTERSON

TAKE YOUR HAT OFF AT THE DINNER TABLE, CALVIN.
HERE COMES THE HURRICANE.
YOU CUT YOUR HAIR!!
NO I DIDN'T. HOBBES DID.
WHY ON EARTH DID YOU CUT YOUR OWN HAIR?! LOOK AT YOU!
I SAID HOBBES CUT IT! YOU THINK I'D DO THIS??
...WELL, I DIDN'T!
WATTERSON

SOME BARBER YOU ARE! MOM SAYS THERE'S NOTHING I CAN DO BUT WAIT FOR MY HAIR TO GROW BACK.
IN THE MEANTIME, I'VE GOT TO GO AROUND LOOKING LIKE I'VE GOT MANGE! I HOPE YOU'RE HAPPY.
HAPPY?! YOU STIFFED ME! WHERE'S MY EIGHT BUCKS?!
!
WATTERSON

LOOK, I'M SORRY I GAVE YOU A BAD HAIRCUT. I DIDN'T MEAN TO.
A FAT LOT OF GOOD THAT DOES ME.
I CAN MAKE IT UP TO YOU. HONEST.
YEAH? HOW?
I BOUGHT A YELLOW MAGIC MARKER.
SEE, I'LL JUST DRAW SOME HAIR ON. THERE, IT'S LOOKING BETTER ALREADY.
REALLY? IS IT?
WATTERSON

WELL, YOUR HAIR DOESN'T STICK UP THE WAY IT USED TO, BUT AT LEAST YOUR HEAD'S YELLOW AGAIN.
THANKS, HOBBES. YOU'RE A REAL LIFE SAVER. I'M SORRY I GOT SO MAD AT YOU.
NONSENSE. NO HARM DONE.
BOY, WAIT TILL I SHOW MOM!
WATTERSON
UH OH. DOES IT COME OFF?
FROM NOW ON, JUST KEEP YOUR BRAINY IDEAS TO YOURSELF, OK?

calvin
calvin the GENIUS
calvin the SUPER GENIUS
THIS IS HOW YOU SIGN YOUR REPORTS?
IT KIND OF INCLINES YOU TO READ IT MORE CHARITABLY, DON'T YOU THINK?
WATTERSON

CLINK
CLINK
MY ICED TEA IS A FAILURE.
WATTERSON

Calvin and HOBBES
by WATTERSON
THIS IS SUPPOSED TO BE GREAT ART.
...SO WHY DOES IT LOOK LIKE A BUNCH OF DECAPITATED NAKED PEOPLE?
A STRANGE FEELING COMES OVER CALVIN IN THE ART MUSEUM.
HIS PARENTS, ENGROSSED IN CULTURE, REMAIN BLISSFULLY UNAWARE OF CALVIN'S TERRIBLE TRANSFORMATION!
YES, A TYRANNOSAURUS IS LOOSE IN THE ART MUSEUM! THE CURATOR SHRIEKS, AND PANDEMONIUM ENSUES!
A GUARD REACHES FOR HIS PISTOL, BUT THE DINOSAUR IS UPON HIM AND HE IS MESSILY DEVOURED!
THE GIANT LIZARD'S GLORY IS CAPTURED FOREVER ON FILM BY THE ANTI-THEFT CAMERAS! PATRONS OF THE ARTS FLEE FOR THEIR LIVES!
HUNDREDS OF PRICELESS PAINTINGS ARE RIPPED TO SHREDS IN THE AWFUL RAMPAGE! WEALTHY BENEFACTORS ARE TRAMPLED! THE MUSEUM IS IN RUINS! ON TO SYMPHONY HALL!!
CALVIN? ... CALVIN? WE'RE IN THE NEXT ROOM NOW. C'MON.
I THINK WE'D BETTER GET HIM OUT OF HERE. HE HAD THAT GRIN AGAIN.
I WANNA SEE THE DINOSAURS AT THE NATURAL HISTORY MUSEUM AGAIN.
WE SPENT ALL AFTERNOON THERE, CALVIN.

The End